DATE DUE

Art Center College of Design
Library
1700 Lida Street
Pasadena, Calif. 91103

X Y Z

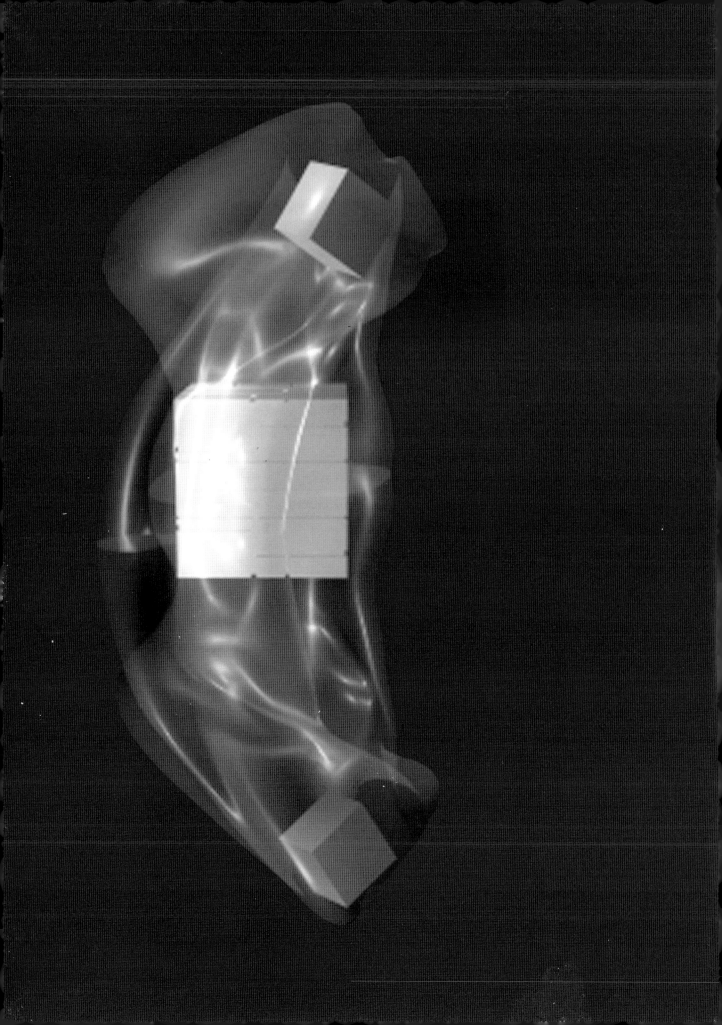

X Y Z

THE ARCHITECTURE OF

DAGMAR RICHTER

PRINCETON ARCHITECTURAL PRESS, NEW YORK

PUBLISHED BY

PRINCETON ARCHITECTURAL PRESS

37 EAST SEVENTH STREET

NEW YORK, NY 10003

FOR A FREE CATALOG OF BOOKS, CALL 1.800.722.6657.

VISIT OUR WEB SITE AT WWW.PAPRESS.COM.

EDITING AND LAYOUT: CLARE JACOBSON

DESIGN: DEB WOOD

COPY EDITING: JENNIFER THOMPSON

SPECIAL THANKS TO: NETTIE ALJIAN, ANN ALTER, AMANDA ATKINS, NICOLA BEDNAREK, JAN

CIGLIANO, JANE GARVIE, MIA IHARA, LESLIE ANN KENT, MARK LAMSTER, NANCY EKLUND LATER,

ANNE NITSCHKE, AND LOTTCHEN SHIVERS OF PRINCETON ARCHITECTURAL PRESS

—KEVIN C. LIPPERT, PUBLISHER

LIBRARY OF CONGRESS CATALOGING-IN-PUBLICATION DATA

RICHTER, DAGMAR, 1955–

   XYZ : THE ARCHITECTURE OF DAGMAR RICHTER.—1ST ED.

     P. CM.

   INCLUDES BIBLIOGRAPHICAL REFERENCES AND INDEX.

   ISBN 1-56898-248-8

     1. RICHTER, DAGMAR, 1955– 2. ARCHITECTURE, MODERN—20TH CENTURY. I. TITLE.

   NA1088.R488 A4 2001

   720'.92—DC21

                                     00-012199

CONTENTS

For Lukas and Elias

ACKNOWLEDGMENTS Architectural design is a collaborative activity. Many people have contributed to the projects published here and have had a tremendous influence on the outcome.

First of all I would like to thank Harvard University and the University of California, Los Angeles as the two institutions that made my academic practice possible, and Peter Cook, who opened my eyes to a world of joy and passion.

In particular, I would like to thank all those who collaborated with me: Ulrich Hinrichsmeyer with a number of projects, Shayne O'Neil with the West Coast Gateway Competition, and Liza Hansen with the New Royal Library, Copenhagen project. Thanks to all those who worked in my studio, among them: Hagy Belzberg, Anna Bolneset, Nick Capelli, Mercedes de la Garza, Justin Dewitt, Michael Filser, Carl Hampson, Marc Kim, Nina Lesser, Joshua Levine, Claudia Lueling, Jonas Luther, Jonathan Massey, Scott Oliver, Tom Robertson, Justin Rumpeles, Behnam Samareh, Carola Sapper, Keith Sidley, Patrick Tighe, Eileen Yankowski, and Theodore Zoumboulakis. None of this work would be where it is without all my students from Harvard University, Columbia University, Art Academy Berlin Weissensee, and especially UCLA. I would like to thank all my colleagues from these and so many other institutions for pushing me further and supporting my work as well as for their willingness to discuss and challenge it.

I would especially like to thank Richard Weinstein for luring me to Los Angeles, Laurie Hawkinson for her generous friendship and hospitality, Regine Leibinger and Frank Barcow for always welcoming me to Berlin, Marc Angelil, Barbara Bestor, Dana Cuff, Neil Denari, Liz Diller, Craig Dykers, Julie Eizenberg, Per Olav Fjeld, Sarah Graham, Michael Hays, Frank Israel, Tom Mayne, Kyong Park, Margie Reeve, Bob Somol, Bernard Tschumi, Toni Vidler, George Wagner, Wilfried Wang, Jane Wernick, and Marc Wigley for their ample advise and their generous support.

I want to say thank you to Claire Zimmerman for giving me a spine when I most needed it and Charlie Frederikson, Lena Hilbertsdottir, and Ulla Skaarup for following up on me and staying in touch with help and friendship through times when I nearly disappeared into the fog. Thanks a million to my research assistants who helped me with this book: Susanne Haeselhoff, Sarah Moylan, and Anthony Guida. Kevin Lippert of Princeton Architectural Press made this book possible in the first place and my editor, Clare Jacobson, made this book not only possible but also certainly a lot better. A special thanks to Toni Vidler for agreeing to be involved in this book.

Last but not least I thank my family, and Peter Baldwin, the father of my two wonderful boys, who shared child-care responsibilities beyond traditional societal expectations. In this respect, this book is dedicated to my two sons, who are the joy of my life.

THE FUTURE IS A GRAPH:
Dagmar Richter's Diagrammatic Practice

ANTHONY VIDLER

"Weak form," "slow space," "the pragmatics of function," "diagrammatic design": such recent characterizations of late modern architecture seem to represent a definitive end of the modernist utopia. In an era when the positive formulations of historical and technological progress seem to be barely sustained by an already fading dot.com marketplace, it has seemed only right to downplay ambition, deny hubris, undersell form, and, in as many ways as possible, counter the modernist image of the architect as hero. Against the more-than-life-size caricatures of Ayn Rand, and the no less caricatural claims of the modern "masters," the last decade has seen an apparent modesty, if not a dissimulation, on the part of practitioners, historians, and theorists as to what we might expect from architecture, formally and socially.

Where, in the 1980s, the perceived problems of modernism were covered over, so to speak, by a postmodern historicism that attempted to apply what was felt to be a richer linguistic repertory, the recent turn has been toward a more restricted palette: transparency replaced by translucency, thickness by thinness, technological exhibitionism by a restrained rhetoric. This is true of hi-tech architecture, with its shift from exhibitionist "inside-out" structures, such as Richard Rogers and Renzo Piano's Pompidou Center or Rogers's Lloyds of London Building, to the reticence of reflective or opaque skins. It is also characteristic of new monuments, such as the half-buried, shuttered enclosure of Daniel Libeskind's Jewish Museum in Berlin, or the more commercial but equally retiring project for the New York Times tower by Piano. Even the new "digital" architecture, with the exception of the explosive rhetoric of Frank Gehry's Guggenheim at Bilbao and subsequent designs, has assumed a signature cast that derives more from the wire-frame construction or the vector map. This sense of "restrained rhetoric," as Roland Barthes called it, extends to the modes of representation adopted for publication that, complex enough in their layered and montaged graphics, nevertheless depend more on the accumulated richness of thin-line transcription than on the simulation of architectonic depth or historical reference.

The affiliation of these new counter-monumental monuments to modernism is evident, and on one level one might explain the movement as a fundamental reaction against an over-exuberant postmodernism. But critics who simply assume this to be a survival or revival of modern movement motifs in an often characterized "late modernism," ignore the fundamental differences in material, method, and form between the two movements. Certainly the new "diagrammatic" architecture has superficial relations to the geometrical forms of modernism. But where modernism's geometries were the result of a language of abstraction, whether materially "realist" or metaphysically idealist, the new diagrams are precisely nothing more nor less than diagrams, not diagrams *of* something, but the something itself. Abstract form has been replaced by delineation. Architects from Rem Koolhaas to Kazuyo Sejima have in this way asserted an affiliation with or allegiance to modernism, while at the same time developing propositions apparently more suited to a more global, yet seemingly less demagogic, condition.

In this movement, the role of the diagram has been hailed as preeminent. "Diagram architecture" is the term coined by Toyo Ito to characterize Sejima's thin-line projects, where the representation of the building as diagram is, so far as possible, translated directly into constructed form. Here critics have drawn relations between diagram architecture and minimalist movements in recent art. But diagrams, as C. S. Peirce noted, are multiple in their forms and functions, and by no means simply minimal communication devices. Indeed in Peirce's terms they are icons that act not as reduced notations but as independent entities operating in parallel and separately from their apparent referents. The richness of the diagram/icon lies precisely in this quasi-utopian role—a form that proposes and projects potential new forms into reality, as opposed to a mere reflection or abstraction of it.

In this context, the complex formal iterations of Dagmar Richter emerge as experimental models pointed towards not a "diagrammatic architecture," but a diagrammatic practice in its own right—a mode of working and a specific set of materials with which to work. Thus the working method can loosely, following Richter's own self-conscious description, be termed "mapping," with its corresponding implications of plotting and projecting. The materials of the method would then be described as "maps" in the most general sense, including graphs, charts, patterns, and the like.

Now of course maps and charts, graphs and diagrams have traditionally been tied to their accurate and representative characteristics with regard to some preexisting reality—the map, for example, that guides a military strategist in plotting a campaign. In architecture, traditional modernist functionalism has been eager to assemble such maps as the data on which a design could be based, and the authentication of this design in relation to the proposed solution. But the example of the military map, one that Peirce himself cites in his demonstration of the iconic nature of mapping, also shows the extensive powers of the map to create its own reality, and even to influence the reality to which it is ostensibly subservient. For, as Peirce points out, a general might know every inch of a given terrain, having walked or observed it from the ground, and yet not know it as the map shows it. The map creates a privileged view, and installs itself as a kind of model for military planning and action, and it is with reference to the map, not the reality, that this action is conceived and carried out. Indeed, as the Gulf War demonstrated, the map was the campaign, whether on the screens of war rooms or individual bombers. For all intents and purposes, the map was the ground of action.

If this kind of substitution is registered in the domain of architecture, as it is in every one of Richter's projects, it is easy to draw the conclusion that in the map, Richter is not simply supplying data for subsequent design, but the material of the design itself. This also means that her "architecture" is not informed by information, but is rather the result of the form of information. Here all notions of a pre-existing "architecture," what Richter calls "a collection of surface images depicting facades of proper historically verified Eurocentric compositions," are overturned in favor of a process that generates structure and form out of non-architectural materials.

This is why the formal results of this process should in no way be confused with what has been erroneously termed "deconstructivist" architecture over the last decade or so. For where "deconstructivism"—whether as presented in the Museum of Modern Art's original exhibition or as extended in reference by critics such as Charles Jencks—took architecture as its starting point (its formal transformations and characteristic decompositions overtly demonstrating architecture's collapse or refabrication), Richter's mapping strategy ignores architecture from the outset, and the end result is entirely disconnected from any known monumental, stylistic, or even imagistic architectural reference. We might indeed be correct in attributing some of the procedures of philosophical deconstruction to her approach—swerving around "architecture," de-stabilizing genres and types sacred to modernism, working with the copy, introducing master metaphors from the outside as formal and procedural precedents—but in essence her method is more structuralist than deconstructivist, dedicated to the investigation of the deep structures of problems, not as they are set, but as they pose themselves.

Thus all the moves involved in Richter's mapping are those of a radical structuralism, such as Ferdinand de Saussure and Claude Levi-Strauss proposed for the analysis of language and culture. Nowhere are these as effective as in the mapping of maps on maps, that process of revealing the conflicts and contradictions inherent in the spatial layering of temporally discrete conditions. Sigmund Freud's (inherently structuralist) observation that "the same space cannot have two different contents" is here tested to its limit, in such a way as to make of it a critical device. For when the same space is forced to comprise multiple spatial contents, revealing their inherent conflicts and contradictions through layering, transparency, translucency, morphing, and transposition, then the result is not so much a denial of the real but a projection of a new real. That is, where Freud was concerned merely to demonstrate the inadequacy of "pictorial terms" to represent the characteristics of mental life (only in the different levels of the mind could the same "space" hold different "contents"), Richter turns the dictum on its head to provoke the production of mental contents out of the confrontation of spatial elements. And rather leading to "things that are unimaginable and even absurd," as in Freud's example of all the previous epochs of ancient Rome literally layered on top of each other, Richter's maps lead to entirely new imaginations. For if a map is an icon that at once represents a mental representation of something, and that independently operates as a mental content in its own right, then the layering of such icons will naturally give rise to what we might term "spatio-mental" constructs—in short, diagrams that are both figures of an alternative architecture and strategies for its conceptualization and mutation.

That this structuralist enterprise is no empty formalism, but what I referred to earlier as a radical structuralism with fundamental political resonance, is indicated in every project by the very selection of mapped worlds. Thus the project for the West Coast Gateway Competition refuses any stable image of what an LA architecture might be. It prefers to resurrect a set of previous forms of inhabitation of the ground, from the geological to the social, in order to propose a mode of inhabitation that both reflects and projects these apparently separate spatial orders into a new form, one that might be called the "unconscious" of the ground. Similarly, the haunted site of the Century City development is excavated in a way that almost filmicly reveals its own transient condition; Beirut is seen through the lens of alternating catastrophe and reconstruction, again figured in multiple maps; and Berlin is reconfigured through its own historical vectors of power and display. In each case the political is figured in the always uncomfortable juxtaposition of competing, often conveniently forgotten, maps of "reality"; in each case a potential new reality is projected from the confrontation. Gilles Deleuze's definition of a diagram, cited by Richter, as "a real that is yet to come, a new type of reality" takes on both political and architectural potency in this context.

In 1960 Reyner Banham attempted to demonstrate the usefulness of historians to designers, stating that "the future is a graph"; by this he meant that the historian's job was to divine the future by referring to the past. He proposed that this future lay in technology, and that, as he stated as the conclusion of *Theory and Design in the First Machine Age*, the architect "to keep up" would have to "discard his whole cultural load, including the professional garments by which he is recognized as an architect." Forty years later, and well into the maturity of the second machine age, the present looks a lot like a graph, or at least a diagram, and the combined operations of

mapping and digitalization have rendered architecture, as traditionally understood, more or less unrecognizable. It is Dagmar Richter's
achievement to have articulated one of the substantial ways in
which the second-machine-age architect, now, not incidentally, in
differently gendered "garments," can demonstrate to the historian
that whatever the future, architecture is not only a graph but a critically transformative one at that.

ANTHONY VIDLER
LOS ANGELES, NOVEMBER, 2000

INTERLEAVINGS AND EXCHANGES:

E-Mail Conversations Between Dagmar Richter and Claire Zimmerman

JANUARY AND MAY 2000

PHOTOS OF DR BY LISBETH HOLT

PHOTOS OF CZ BY CHRISTOPHER RATTÉ

RE-SKINNING

[cz] The word "re-skinning" comes up in a variety of projects, related to the specific conditions of each one. It clearly represents a larger strategy linked to a particular commitment on your part, bigger than any specific project.

[DR] Yes, it is bigger and represents a basic strategy—mostly body-related, dedicated, physical, and authored (*and* optimistic).

[cz] Nevertheless, it is also possible to interpret "re-skinning" relative to the individual projects and their contexts. Then it emerges as ameliorative, as an effort to reflect or even repair a diagnosed "pathology," and can be linked both to organicism and to a notion of healing. This is perhaps not what you mean by it, but the implication is there. Perhaps we can explore this a little.

[DR] I know that ameliorative intents seem passé in contemporary architectural practice. Isn't it still the case that architecture is mainly based on thorough destruction and ample denial of cultural and physical contexts in order to be recognized as novel and avant-garde? At least that is what I hear every day as a teacher and in most of the stars' lectures.

[cz] Passé or not, I'd like to know more about this, and what is being ameliorated, specifically (I can imagine but would like to hear it from you). How is the notion of amelioration linked to the feminine? How can this link convincingly be made? Perhaps here you will refer me to Hélène Cixous et al?

[DR] Yes, Cixous was quite important to me. I remember reading her when I was barely into architecture and thought I'd better write plays or movie scripts. She discussed the overall problem to start writing and creating—being simultaneously conscious about one's own position as a new member in this reluctant community. In her text "Utopias," which was translated in the book *New French Feminisms* (edited by Elaine Marks and Isabelle Courtivron) she wrote, "Where woman has never her turn to speak—this being all the

more serious and unpardonable in that writing is precisely *the very possibility of change, the space that can serve as a springboard for subversive thought, the precursory movement of a transformation of social and cultural structures."* I read these texts with great interest since they gave me a possibility to create and design. She wrote a lot about writing from one's body—from a world of searching on the basis of systematic experimentation. Re-skinning may have come from there (but also could be read as an outcome of my being rather uncomfortable in my own skin after I entered the profession).

[cz] **This last aside—about comfort in one's own skin. This introduces the question of self and other, which is highly relevant to a discussion of your work. Specifically, there is one sense in which these projects might be discussed as projections of a female body onto or into a site and program, and another in which they might be discussed as terrains subject to the activities of a female consciousness. The difference has to do with projection into or action upon. Where the first might be**

thought as a distinctly female trope, the latter is certainly the more conventional model, where the architect—as surgeon, say—acts on his subject (clients, site, program, etc.). What makes discussing your work so interesting is trying to understand your way of projecting, and how the female body—itself acted upon, prostheticized, contaminated, impinged upon—actually becomes a metaphor for the work.

BODY DIAGNOSIS

[cz] **So to turn to the Los Angeles projects, "re-skinning" Los Angeles would seem to mean giving back a surface (indicating a wholeness?) to a city without any "body" to speak of. How is the notion of "re-skinning" pertinent here?**

[DR] Los Angeles does not need more surfaces (how deep can we go?). It has a body, a more female one, a body without history—light, fleeting, slightly angst ridden where age is concerned, afraid of age and therefore in constant need of a quick cosmetic fix.

[cz] And do the projects proposed for Los Angeles address this body? If so, I am led immediately to the idea of a kind of cosmetic "fix" in the case of the West Coast Gateway Competition. But perhaps a more general point could be made here in terms of the initial site reading (or "context analysis"). I think you are suggesting a way of reading the feminine—a way of reading the formerly unread, as it were—within the conventional task of site analysis.

I understand you to mean that feminism is in part simply an act of reading. In Louis Sullivan's view, the "feminine" exists everywhere, waiting only to be recognized. But while this notion is appealing in a sort of pseudomystical way (like many of Sullivan's odd notions), it perhaps isn't quite adequate for our purposes. One can simply *read* as a feminist, as Cixous and others do; this seems to me to describe your activity well. For architects this act of reading is, of course, the principle preliminary act—prior to all decision-making or designing. The notion of "re-skinning" itself rests on a particular kind of reading, on

diagnosis—your diagnosis of the problem, whether it be specifically site-related or more generally conceived. Here the figure of the nurse-architect emerges right at the outset.

[DR] I am looking for the unread feminine in a public body and social body. I want to appropriate and play with authority. Don't you think, today more than ever, that quasi-scientific procedures and an insistence on an absolute rationalism have been called to perform the role of authorization in many planners' and architects' processes? The permanent breaking down of the intended composition through the use and appropriation of the users seems to be seen as a fundamental threat to the discipline. Our first exercises around 1988 questioned the authority of the design process. We dealt with the feminist critique of the traditional definition of composition, the site's presumed lack of identity, and the author's cultural authority to organize and normalize society's desires. Many of us women were newcomers, safely placed at the margins. Many of us had to experience at any panel discussion at any conference at any possi-

ble invitation to speak on our behalf, that the few invitations were mostly an opportunity to ignore us at the events and make sure that it was made clear from the beginning that we were only there because society needed a women for the photographs. How many times did I sit on a panel where there were on average twelve to fourteen men and me placed safely most left in the margins? As active designers we women were always outside, at least in academia. Since we always return from afar, from without, from "the heath where witches are kept alive" (Cixous), the very act of designing toward and from a new body definition is quite exciting and pleasurable.

ON "THE PRACTICE OF LAUGHTER"
(SINCE CIXOUS IS ON OUR MINDS RIGHT NOW)

[cz] Beirut "re-skinned." There is an obvious condition of healing appropriate to Beirut.

[DR] Here the original profession of the nurse-architect is important. Do you think it is too traditionally female?

[cz] Certainly not—but I think it is remarkably idealistic and very much against any current stream in architecture. I think the more female it can be the better—at least in terms of defining a feminist practice in architecture. This has to be done both radically and thoughtfully. Not only is the potential for either ridicule or further marginalization huge, there is also a lack of consensus about how to be a feminist, or how to be feminist, particularly in this field. Neither the overtly feminine nor the pretense at a potentially ungendered practice is workable. In particular, I don't see the point of establishing oneself as a sort of pale echo of the male power structure. You have intentionally never done this, although you complain about being outside that structure frequently. I find the idea of the nurse-architect quite compelling, as long as we're talking as much Nurse Ratched as Florence Nightingale—if that's possible.

The nurse-architect emerges as a counter to our discussion below of the two fictional "heroines" O and V. That is, the first case involves a vesting of power through control over the body—the body of another—as opposed to the divestment of

power over the body—the body of the self—in the second two cases. In the case of Nurse Ratched (*One Flew Over the Cuckoo's Nest*), this is of course power over the mind of others through power over their bodies. Interestingly, this is a demonic power. I can't offhand think of an example of this sort of power vested in a woman that is not then demonized. Can you?

[DR] Maybe the nymphet type of Marguerite Duras?

[cz] So two feminine models—power through seduction, or power through domination? I think there must be another way, perhaps leaving the question of power entirely aside. The first choice of the politically marginalized. Detour. But for the moment, can we hold this dyad—the nurse-architect ministering to the weakened body of the other, versus the sexualized body surrendering itself to forces from without?

POLITICS AND BERLIN

[cz] Berlin "re-skinned" has some similarities to Beirut, though of course more remote in time. Here you "re-skinned" a city that skinned (cut of

its own skin) itself between 1943 and 1945. But the language is tricky here—"to skin" means to remove the skin; to "re-skin" ought then to mean removing the skin a second time. You are using the term to designate the replacement of skin (even prosthetically)—quite the opposite meaning. In fact, both meanings have some relevance to this discussion.

[DR] Berlin is pretty raw—it lost civility and culture. It is a very fascinating city to be involved in, but ultimately truly frustrating. What Walter Benjamin wrote on Berlin in 1929 still holds true. In "Die Wiederkehr des Flaneur," he accused Berlin of being uneasy with the idea of being a capital, since it did not want to be confronted as a transitional space of all knowable forces.

[cz] So the lost skin of Berlin is the lost skin of civility and culture, and it represents some loss of nerve in the face of modern urban identity. It must also be the lost skin of a kind of moral certainty, not to mention self-respect. This is all recorded in your response, I think. But perhaps you could be more explicit.

[DR] I felt it was urgent to react politically and seriously try to find a way to steer architecture back to the political. When I came to the United States, I realized that architecture under the circumstances of rampant (not state-controlled) capitalism had lost the discipline's intellectual edge because it surrendered its own political content to commercial commodity production, pure and simple. This at least can be seen since Philip Johnson's first transformation of ideology towards style at the modernist show at the Museum of Modern Art in New York in 1932. Re-rendering modernism not as a social movement but as a style certainly did the trick. Are we not now specifically confronted with the definition of architectural design as form-play and architectural discourse as sophisticated play? How do we react today hearing the words "affect" and "performance" over and over again? How do we contain our political convictions and serious social concerns in the design? We tried new methodologies in the Proposal for a New Government Center in Berlin. We experimented with the automatic superficial authority of the male single author. We

"sang in a chorus" (from the antique Greek plays, which reminds me of those scenes in Woody Allen's movie *Everybody Says I Love You*).

[cz] Could you elaborate a little more here? How in fact does one lodge architecture in the political? I know how it was done in the twenties and thirties, and I think I have an idea how it was done in Britain and even Europe in the sixties and seventies. But in terms of present production, I am lost. How have you done this?

[DR] I can only say that to remain in the political cannot be depicted in the formal outcome of a distinct style. It is more engrained in the methodologies of production—in an attempt to use architecture as an art of resistance. You could study the processes involving new definitions of authorship. One might see it in our use of site not as a neutral entity but as a contaminated text. Also one might see it in our attempts to allow the design to be contaminated, since we expected the design to be appropriated by the next user-reader.

[cz] So to the act of diagnosis we add an act of mimesis—that what is found in the conditions of the project is incorporated into the designer's brief. This is a fairly extreme version of contextualism, where diagnosis becomes the process of design as well. Is this germane to the idea of a feminist architecture?

[DR] At least I could say that feminist theory demands radical contextualism, since in a nutshell everything is there already and everything lies in the commentary.

ABOUT MOTHER NATURE

[cz] The Shanghai Residential Design 2000 Competition presents a different model, because here "re-skinning" has to do with the recreation of landscape, with appreciation of the preindustrial culture of China. This design strategy appears as a naturalist response, returning surface to topography. In that sense, it is less specific to a particular city and more pertinent to a discussion of landscape and architecture. But if we use the term "re-skinning" here as well, it begins to seem a versatile strategy. It also opens up the further question of grafting, and of simulation, in a sense.

[DR] After we redefined our design process the clear distinction between proper architecture and "passive, female" landscape did not make sense any more. By trying to reread the cultural products (once more but with feeling) with our eyes, other hierarchies started to emerge. We realized that all these constructs—be they landscape or architecture—are highly artificial and we did not respond with propriety to the given historic precedents, which we started to question.

V AND O

[cz] I don't mean to read your work too literally. That is, these new "skins" are all, as I understand them, complex, highly artificial ensembles of

constructed matter. So they are grafts, mecha-
nized substitutes for whatever condition they are
diagnosing, imitating, or ameliorating.

[DR] "Re-skinning" does not refer to surface at all. The
movie *Powers of Ten* by Ray and Charles Eames
comes to mind. It is and stays a question of scale
and, in my case, of a point of view.

[cz] This is an elusive comment. You are then substi-
tuting a notion of area for one of surface. The sig-
nificance of this presumably has to do with
avoiding any formal restrictions, in terms of how
the projects will develop. Through this reference
you are also adding a notion of relativity, which
seems to have been implicit from the beginning.
But not to digress too far from the subject of the
graft, or the prosthesis…

[DR] There is something there about the artificiality of
the cyborg character—Donna Haraway?

[cz] In terms of other models than the cyborg model, I
asked you some time ago about the Thomas

Pynchon book, *V*, because of the gradual transformation in that book of V, the main character,
from a nineteenth-century woman into a sort of
twentieth-century prosthetic machine. This construct could be important for our discussion.
Also, there is the main character in *The Story of
O*, who gradually transforms herself or is transformed into an object for sexual pleasure,
including various physical alterations—perhaps
(apocryphally) written by a housewife in France
in the 1950s—have you read it? Both these novels
document the transformation of the female body
by various forces, thus presenting it as an incom-
plete, mutable body, a continual work in
progress. The process of "re-skinning," or
restoring skin to raw places, can be understood
in these terms—as a projection of the changing
female body, one that adjusts itself in response
to the demands placed upon it. I am of course trying to suggest that there is a metonymic relationship between your projects and the continually
vulnerable feminine body. The design process
then has something to do with replacement—
with the substitution of artificial material for

organic matter. This seems to me an important polemical point, one that constitutes an important point of discussion for a feminist practice.

[DR] Rather, substitution of artificial material for artificial material. I think we get into quicksand where the definition of the organic (nature?) is concerned. What is fascinating about *The Story of O* is how the female is reconstructed as a vessel—fast, accessible, and empty. I was never interested in this model since it always rendered the female void of culture herself. But are we not moving toward this particular definition for architecture (her) today? That leaves the prosthesis as a model for me, since it is not about voiding out—to the contrary this process of design is providing an authored graft and dedicated prosthesis. Tentatively spoken, though.

I have to go back a bit. I have to remind myself that I did read Mark Wigley's article on the prosthesis in *Assemblage*. I do not want to further the modernist idea of architecture as woman's body replacement. I am not interested in prosthesis as a historical military device, as in "arms." That is why the word "skin" is important here, since skin grafts are an art to direct growth within, not to replace parts. How is our relationship to nature today different from that of the modernists? The modernists protected themselves from the organic—looked at it through the glass plane—safely framed and tamed. (Safely framing Josephine Baker, for example, and the women in the photographs of Le Corbusier's villas, or Marcel Duchamp's *Large Glass*.) Now this frame has shifted considerably. Nature has suddenly moved into architecture; it throbs and pulsates through the provided spaces via uncontrollable masses—now male and female—that appropriate and act upon it. A number of new professions have been developed around mass control, for example. The datascapes need to tame masses now from within. I think it is not possible to tame it safely; not even by employing the ultimate machine, the computer, will the unpredictable reality of life be controllable. I also deem it undesirable.

O's obvious existential pleasure in her transformation is interesting. I see this as an overall cultural fantasy—not solely female. O is whipped not only to transform her skin but also to empty her out of any preconceived notion of her own identity and history. That always made women desirable—I guess as cities and projects are for many architects. Isn't this the ultimate modern architect's fantasy? But if the city is "V" (all females are reduced to single letters since we have no name as vessels). If the modernist dream of turning her into a pure predictable machine feels closer today, then this is only because datascape propagandists—ultimately the outcome of neo neo-modernists—are still trying to tame, frame, and void her of any cultural resistance. By the way, Gilles Deleuze seems to be superficially translated and thinned to a very unconvincing formalism by the time he hits the architect's desks. I understand Deleuze more in the direction of Michel De Certeau—things needing to be alive and politically active. I see woman (that is, city) as an organism that is quite unpredictable, which produces a lot of pain in many architect's minds.

Now architects are cloning also. Berlin, for example, would be quite happy to just clone itself since its cultural and ideological convictions have been weakened. On rare occasions, mainly involving Holocaust architecture, Berlin resorts to sensationalist projects, since then it at least can say it listened to and solicited from its rescuers' strategies. It seems that the absence of ideology only leaves two ways out: sensation of the novel or cloning.

[cz] **Just to return to O and V for a moment. O provides a relatively clear case and, I agree with you, an overall cultural fantasy, potentially not only female (although often female—think of anorexia, self-mutilation, etc.). But V is a more complicated case. As well as I can remember, V is both a woman and a concept—that is, an emblem of gradual loss of body, disintegration of the organic in favor of an increasingly crafted set of prostheses, or of an organic past, gradually dismembered or eviscerated by the twin beasts of colonialism and cataclysm (world war),**

emerging alternately as immensely powerful and totally defenseless. This more complex depiction of a feminine agency seems worth discussing, both on its own terms and in its historical framework. And V is certainly mostly a kind of authoritative creature, or notion, in that book. If what we are looking for is authority (you know my doubts on that subject), V is like an enigmatic cross between Nurse Ratched and O, and so a cross between the self-perversion of the nymphet and the controlling demonism of the nurse-architect.

THE PAST

[cz] "Re-skinning" clearly does not refer back to an urban condition predating a particular historical event. That is, cities do not consist of skins—they are projections into depth, not surfaces. So the "re" part of "re-skinning" seems to refer to a topographical condition, returning the highly urban to the topographical, to a condition of surface—or area—related to earth surface.

[DR] This has to do with the idea that my design may have a perverse and totally contaminated relationship to precedents, therefore looking for landscape skin. As a woman, I can't believe in precedents' particular value.

[cz] I don't fully understand this. I understand that a perverse, contaminated relationship to precedents leaves one looking for a topographic skin instead of creating a skyscraper city. But what is it that you can't believe in?

[DR] The skyscraper city does not have a perverse relationship—it is perfectly happy to suppress history to the unconscious. This never produces an open recognition of perversion—not even to Walter Benjamin, when he so clearly recommends to erase history in order to be able to prepare for the future. I think the idea of perversion first came through the postmodernists and particularly through the French feminists in the sixties and seventies.

[cz] Are you then suggesting that the desire for a perverse and totally contaminated relationship to
precedents leads back to nature? So then the
topographical interest emerges from a kind of
negative decision? You choose landscape
because you can't choose any building precedents? I don't buy this, because it seems to me
that those aren't really the two choices, or at
least not the only two choices, as you yourself
have shown by looking at sponges and skins and
things. Also, why a "perverse and totally contaminated relationship to precedents"?

[DR] Oh no, don't get me wrong about my supposed
return to nature—it's not even remotely possible.
I think perversion is a good metaphor here—it is
not at all neutral and certainly deals with precedents, not fleeing to nature. I just hope that it
does not diminish the work into a retreat into a
neutralized world void of precedents. But my relationship to precedents certainly reflects the feminists' critique of Jacques Lacan. We do need a bit
of perversion here in order to go forward. The
pleasure in this is obvious. Not only was hysteria
suggested as a methodology, it was also sug-

gested that we ought to pun outrageously as
well as play to subvert the Lacanian principle of
order. So hopefully this is not a retreat but a pleasurable system of experimentation with topography as well as precedents. I hope that these
formal manipulations will eventually weave spatial conditions as socially effective for aspects of
daily life.

MESHWORKS

[cz] I can see the idea of a meshwork relative to your
writing. I also see that the relationship of this
particular image/tactical entity to its feminist
foundation is important, presumably because of
both the flexibility and relative invisibility of a
mesh, and also its ubiquity. This is a more specific typological or just constructional reference
than we have had before, obviously pertinent
to any discussion of grafts or skins. Your
"Meshworks" is a description of a political/tac-
tical position, and is thus a very different kind of
text than the others. It seems to me a kind of surreptitious manifesto. But the title (more than the
description at the moment) is directly (visually,

conceptually) linked to the discussion of surface, skin, layering, topography, etc. So it seems a particularly provocative opportunity. I assume this is all perfectly intentional and worked out on your part—a forceful metaphor for a feminist practice. Like all manifestos, it requires clarity (and some exaggeration) for the proper punch.

[DR] What about this: "Any act of reading is simultaneously an act of appropriation, and the selection of reading material is crucial in order to arrive at a relevant spatial representation. Our art of architecture has been developed as a strategy of copy, recombination, appropriation, trickery, and rhetoric of use. A new meshwork finally starts to occur when directional vectors, sizes of speed, and variables of time are interwoven. This space can influence action but never define it." (I wrote that once when I was supposed to write a manifesto.) In one way or another I do not think that we are at a time of forceful (often translated into "easy understandable") manifestos, yet it plays so well into the consumer practice of the commercial publication industry—at least if one doesn't seriously consider one's practice an academic one.

[cz] I am interested in the idea of a covert operation, or a kind of surreptitious practice, skirting around the other practices within which you must navigate. So to your description of the tokenism of women in conferences and panel discussions, I read the idea of that token as an active agent of subversion in some way. Is this carried out in your practice?

[DR] Yes. To quote Michel de Certeau on Clausewitz, "Power is bound by its very visibility. In contrast, trickery is possible for the weak, and often it is his only possibility, as a 'last resort.'...The weaker the forces at the disposition of the strategist, the more the strategist will be able to use deception. I translate: the more the strategy is transformed into tactics." Also let us remember Ann Bergren's plea for metis, the tactic of deception by the weak.

[cz] I don't know if I believe in that as a strategy for women on a political level—there are problems with it in many cases. I guess I prefer the idea of the amazon—scarred but made for fighting.

[DR] I came to the conclusion that it is possible to subvert in the most pleasurable way. The idea to practice laughter, the idea of the pleasure to write in white ink (mother's milk), the idea of the pun, and the idea of the laughing mother by the French feminists has always given me a tremendous push. It provides quite a positive model of authorship. The readers, the consumers, and the weak ones in the system also have been rendered lately as rather subversive. "They trace 'indeterminate trajectories'...theory moves toward the indeterminate, while technology moves toward the functionalist distinction" (de Certeau wrote this). So we can pun, appropriate, and have fun. Instead of following the classical idea that a process of invention and composition defines the act of designing and assigning, I venture to propose that one has to regard oneself as an editing specialist who critically initiates choice through a process of translation of already assembled material. This involves a lot more strategic thinking and may not be that visible at first, since it uses the margins consciously and plays and experiments with precedence, until new diagrams emerge that point forward.

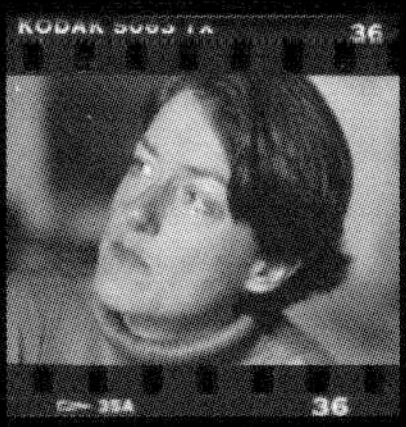
36
35A
36

1 PRODUCED IN 1988
Principals: Dagmar Richter
and Shayne O'Neil
Assistant: Thomas Robertson

2 "Point of departure: rejection of existing information, zero dimension. Followed by the amassing of new data, assessment, and choice. The anatomy of form is studied, vectors are built, earth measurements and scale factors rearranged, grid systems created, and dimensions added. And when the perfect form slowly emerges, it is carefully obliterated, dissected, and pulled apart, not only to find further beauty but to gain other perspectives." Jill Hartz, ed., *Agnes Denes* (New York: Cornell University and Herbert F. Johnson Museum of Art, 1992), 84.

3 Los Angeles first made its mark on me with the typical violence and vastness it has continued ever since. During my first visit in 1988, an earthquake rocked me gently at first and then decisively pushed me out of bed. With my hosts Sarah Graham and Marc Angelil, I spent the rest of the damp, cool morning sitting on a perfectly manicured simulated grass lawn listening to the sound of thousands of car alarms and the smooth flow of traffic permanently floating around us.

4 "Commonly, Europeans took the absence of written maps as an endorsement of the 'emptiness' of the land, as further evidence of its lack of 'cultivation.' Unmapped land was land unoccupied, and to that extent unpossessed. The 'uncharted' territories that Europeans mapped commonly already had their maps, complex oral maps embedded in genealogy, legend and ideology, and sustained by memory and ritual, which took literary rather than visual form. The inscribed map registered and itself hastened dispossession, replacing and silencing what had gone before." Wystan

RESKINNING THE CITY

"*Map Projections* enters art in the form of process, involving the pleasures of doing—shaping, transforming, splitting, erasing, and the excitement of the search, the hunt, the analysis, the discovery."[2]

With the West Coast Gateway Competition, my studio entered a new phase of sincere questioning in which we attempted for the first time to engage in a redefinition of the concept of authorship. The loss of our belief in an intimate connection between an avant-garde production and unprecedented individual invention made Los Angeles an obvious choice. Its particular relationship to a short and highly transformative urban history gave us ample opportunity to revisit our own ideology of architectural history as a collection of surface images depicting facades of proper historically verified Eurocentric compositions.[3] So, from the libraries of Cambridge, Massachusetts we searched for stories and local maps of Los Angeles to ground a process of discursive interpretation among several participants.[4]

Curnow, "Mapping and the Expanded Field of Contemporary Art," in Denis Cosgrove, ed., *Mappings* (London: Reaction Books, 1999), 254.

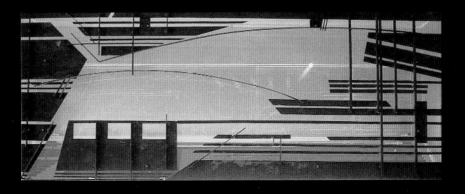

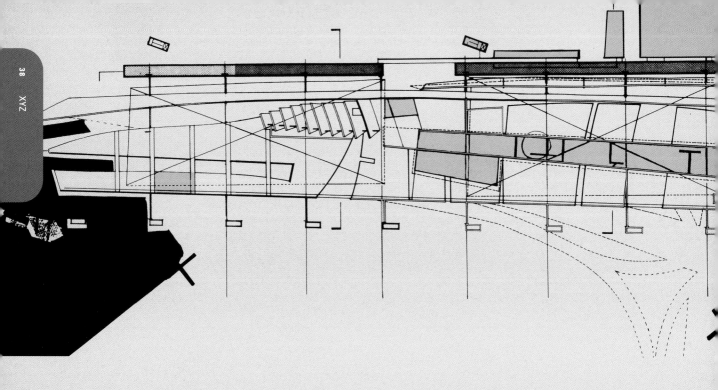

The competition brief requested proposals to reclaim public space above a segment of an eight-lane freeway that cut a deep physical and social scar into the downtown fabric. In this atypical site, it was difficult, at first, to establish an urban context beyond the immediate activities. The organizers wanted the proposed solution to be a symbol, very much like the Statue of Liberty, to serve as a monument for the immigrant groups who had contributed to the prosperity of Los Angeles. In the absence of a functional program, we chose to appropriate this space for the public at large, and for social services for new immigrants arriving in Los Angeles, none of whom have a collective image with which to identify.[5]

Site photograph

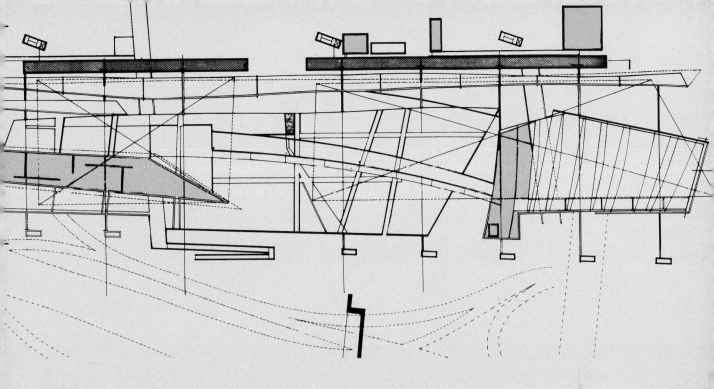

The local geological maps we obtained were from different time periods, revealing a messy, hidden layering of contradictory orders. The unpredictable reality of permanent change and fluidity that defines Los Angeles served as an inspiration and provided the basis for a series of compositional studies and abstractions. We did not endorse the normally perceived authority of found maps as verified objective precedence, which limits space-finding to a distilled archaeology of the immediate site and its urban context. To the contrary, we used the maps to construct interpretations, to contaminate the site with found materials and our own narratives, and to depart from the inevitable grid ideology and its idealized ordering systems.[6]

5 The intellectual and invigorating atmosphere at the Harvard GSD, where I taught at the time, invoked our discursive questioning. It became an uneasy task to create a symbol for diversity without invoking great fear in calling upon the established cultural hegemonies. The people directly involved in this process were Shayne O'Neill as my design partner and Tom Robertson as an assistant. Marc Angelil, Caroline Constant, Laurie Hawkinson, Michael Hays, Kevin Kieran, George Wagner, Wilfried Wang, and Marc Wigley were all at the GSD at the time and always eager for debate. I am forever grateful for this intellectually charged time, which was sternly observed and held together by Raphael Moneo.

6 We found traces of Native American trails, the irrigation channels of the missions, and fragmentary layouts of orange groves—the first organized ordering systems for development from the time the site was still regarded as landscape. We deciphered the first established block structures, built after 1900, and a later collapse of smaller buildings from the gold rush era. A redevelopment of dense downtown block structures was re-aestheticized by the City Beautiful Movement. Finally, a total demolition was employed to cut the immense freeway-system into the city fabric.

Site photograph

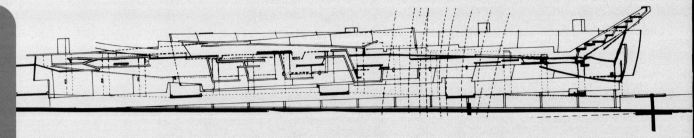

When we began design work for this competition, I was still inspired by a project I had recently completed with a friend in Germany under the group name MAX; 1,2. It became a springboard for this new process.

Our investigation of the processes of sedimentation on the site suggested several layers directly linked to various historical site conditions. Maps of paths, irrigation channels, field boundaries, and building volumes were integrated into a spatial reading in which all layers of map representations were read simultaneously. This dictated an array of interpretations resulting in a new three-dimensional composition containing crevices, volumes, and fields. These layers were read as abstract patterns that could change in meaning through the design and interpretation process, and particularly through their intended use.

Footnote Project: Berlin 3
In this project, we used the techniques of rap music to create an angry project questioning the political control that high art in Berlin exercised to maintain the status quo. We defied the proper use of precedence by stealing, copying, and falsifying found compositions in architecture, painting, and sculpture from Berlin in order to provoke a set of drawings and models depicting a third Berlin that, through its simulated existence, was supposed to contribute to the collapse of the division of the East and West German territories.

Little did we know that soon after, the exact popular copy of culture for easy consumption on television actually provoked the collapse of the wall.
Project Credits:
Produced in 1986
Principals: Dagmar Richter and Ulrich Hinrichsmeyer

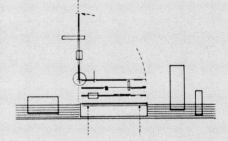

The most elevated abstract layer, representing Los Angeles's hard asphalt surfaces penetrated by building volumes, was rotated into a vertical orientation. This transformation, from horizontal to vertical, generated a layered wall system, a series of surfaces, protecting sensitive areas from the highway's hazards.

This intended skin graft over the scar of the freeway presents conscious veneer architecture, indicating a certain independence of skin and structure. The horizontally layered platforms and volumes above the freeway were to provide spaces in which temporary, exceptionally public programs would reclaim a pedestrian domain presently allocated to the automobile. For the over-one-million daily drivers on the freeway, the underside would display the layers of the abstracted landscapes above in all of their three-dimensionality and would produce a play of light and shadow as one drove by.

I will not give up...

until I have found the Potsdamer Platz.

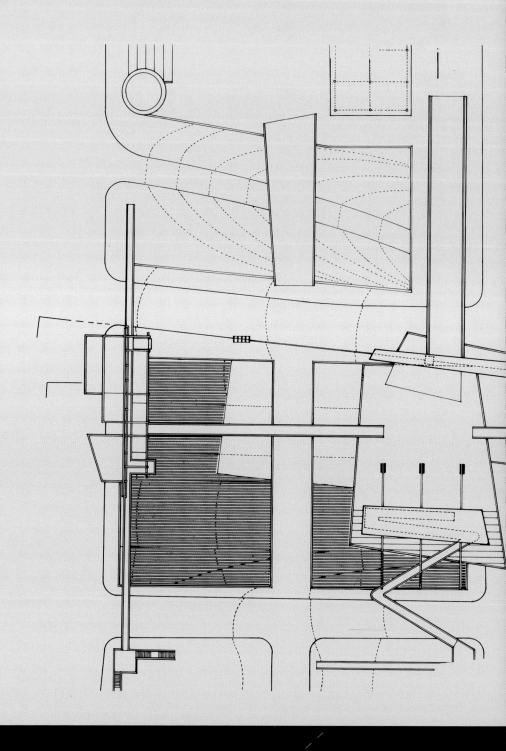

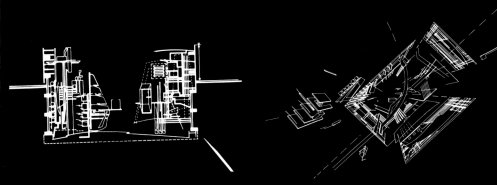

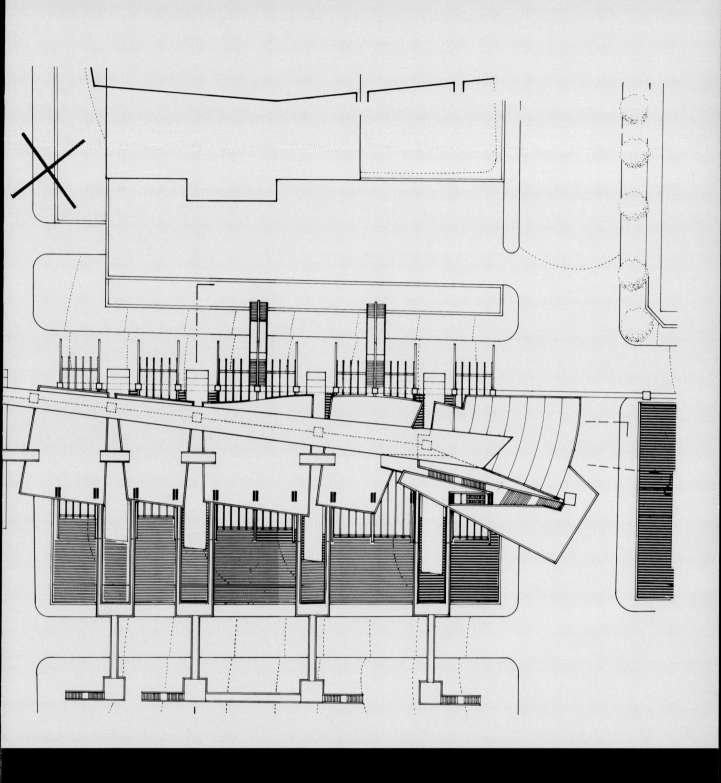

Berlin 3
left: Drawings
right: Working model

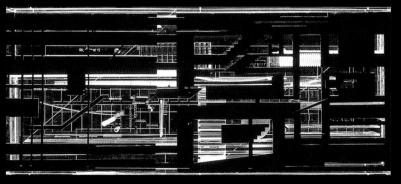

In the second phase of the project,[7] my studio was confronted with a new set of information.[8] Therefore, our interests shifted toward constructive possibilities that defined new relationships between different layers of structures, surfaces, and volumes. With the help of our engineering office, we assigned each layer a specific constructive, environmental, and functional role and gave it a distinct position within the section. The new requirements gave us the opportunity to readdress the issue of meaning with regard to the different maps we found. Each layer was composed through a re-representation of map features found in the geological maps, which dated from the beginning of the twentieth century onwards. The lowest layer carried a thin layer of waterfalls, and was assigned the function of cleaning the air and providing a permanent acoustic screen of white noise. A second, "soft" layer carried moss-like landscape elements and was positioned on top of the "water" layer. We used found "hard" surface compositions to design a pedestrian surface for public gatherings and events on top of the "soft" layer. Volumes penetrating the three surfaces carried informational, electrical, and water infrastructures, as well as provisions for events including fold-out elements for temporary markets and food vendors. Finally, different layers positioned along the freeway folded up and hinged vertically to create smaller, more intimate indoor program elements at each end.

7 Competition entry for the West Coast Gateway Competition, Phase 2: Third Prize Produced in 1988
Principals: Dagmar Richter and Shayne O'Neil
Assistants: David Adler, Roger Fairey, Eric Lum, Anthony Poon, and Thomas Robertson
Engineers: Ove Arup and Partners
Project Engineer: Jane Wernick
Contact Architects in LA: Ansehn & Allen
Project Architect: Sarah Dennison

8 Little did we know that this entire enterprise was mainly organized by the Presidential election campaign manager for Mike Dukakis, who used this competition to increase public relations with the immigrant population and to inspire the voting immigrants to side with him in the upcoming election. Many technological and financial constraints were imposed despite the fact that no construction funds were available.

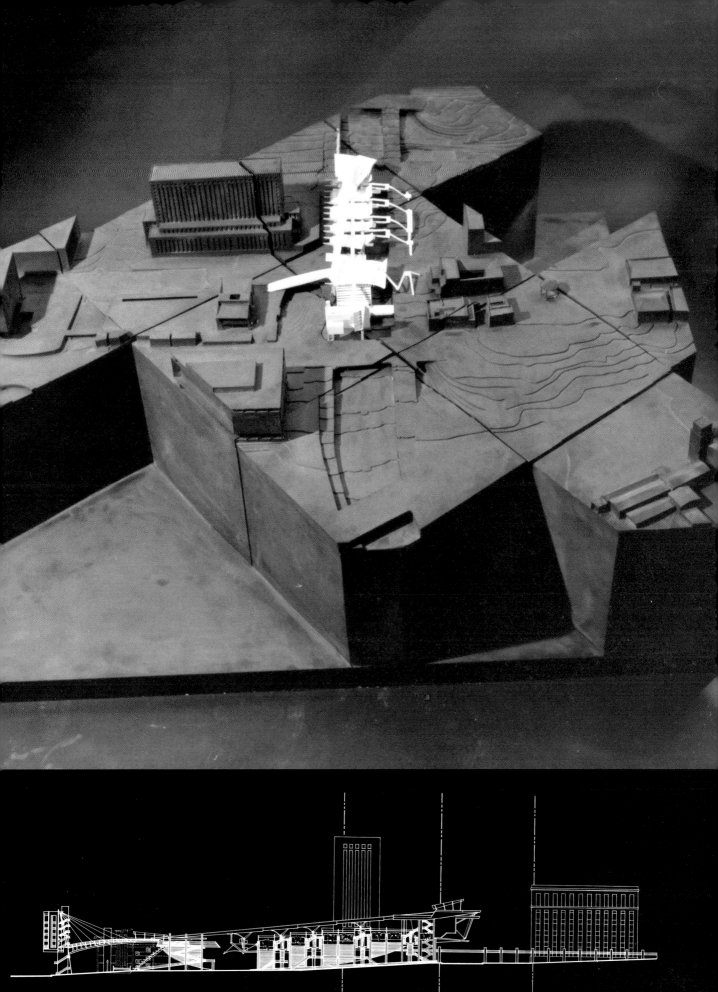

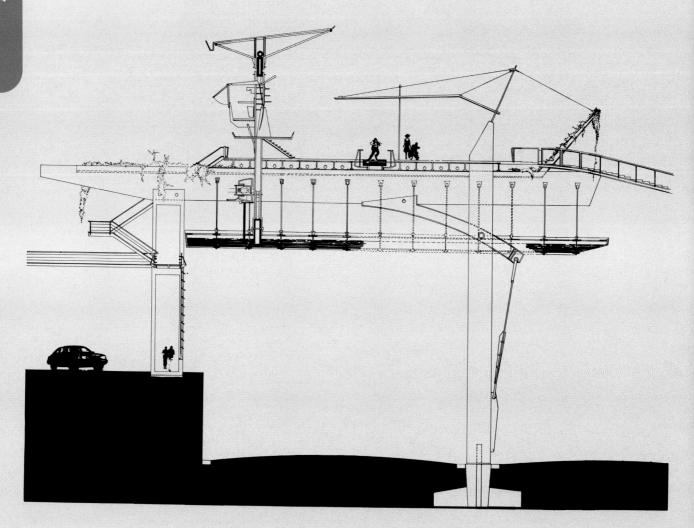

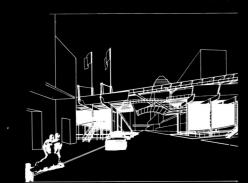

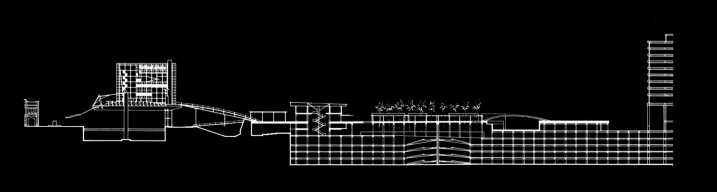

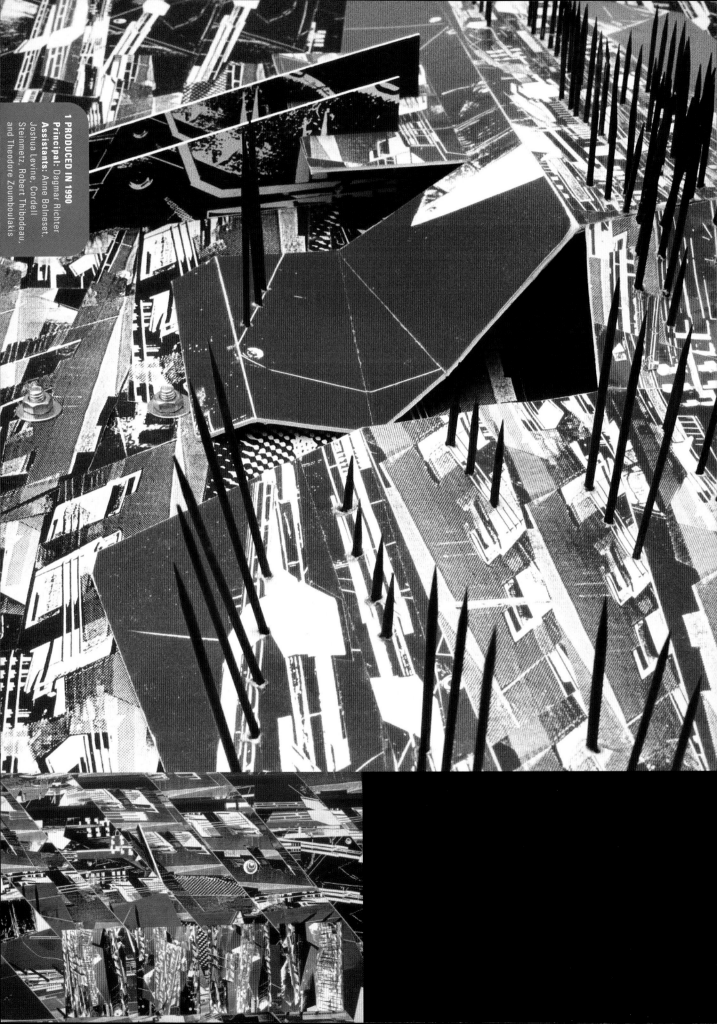

1 PRODUCED IN 1990
Principal: Dagmar Richter
Assistants: Anne Bolneset,
Joshua Levine, Cordell
Steinmetz, Robert Thibodeau,
and Theodore Zoumboulakis

OVERCODING

DESIGN AS TRANSLATION[2]

By the end of the 1980s, the design process of my studio had been effectively redefined by a small and relatively consistent group interested in the transformations permitted by a continuous exchange of individual architectural representations. Hierarchies became blurred.[3] The resultant process became dependent on the different metaphorical transformations, translation techniques, and codes of representation enacted by the contributors. We considered classical concepts regarding the structural hierarchy of cultural definitions, orders, engineering, and construction. The distinction between building (as cultural artifact, masculine, sovereign, and dominating) versus landscape (as natural, feminine, submissive, and passive) became more fluid. The hierarchy of structure over surface and ornament became irrelevant, as these elements now stood parallel in a non-hierarchical field of fragments.

2 This text is presented here in an edited form, from my article Dagmar Richter, "Reading Los Angeles: A Primitive Rebel's Account," *Assemblage* 14 (April 1991), 66–81.
3 My studio operated with the help of my students, or research assistants. I formulated methodologies and experimental frameworks, which were then used as a guideline for further experimentation. I had just left Harvard to teach at UCLA and was awarded a small faculty research grant to conduct this research.

In 1990, we chose Century City, a modernist commercial development in Los Angeles, as a site for speculation. Before 1958, Century City was the site where Twentieth Century Fox Film Studios had constructed and stored an array of simulated environments; entire cities and lakes were made to order. When the studios faced near bankruptcy in the late 1950s, after the box office disaster *Cleopatra*, developers and studio chairman S. P. Skouras hired Welton Becket to create a concept that would transform the back lot of this dream factory into a futuristic city and, therefore, rescue the film industry via real-estate transactions. Planners envisioned a total community anchored by a strong business base. As a result of their efforts, we are today presented with a "prestigious address for business, shopping, luxury living, theater going, dining, and guest accommodation."[4] Century City stands as an ideal outcome of modernist planning and formal ideology, with an emphasis on cleanliness, open spaces, and verticality, a car-oriented infrastructure, and independence from the rest of the city.

4 Century City is described by the local Chamber of Commerce as a landmark for modern urban development. It houses 2500 businesses, 40,000 employees, 4000 residences, 1600 hotel rooms, 150 stores, and is air conditioned and heated by more than 40,000 gallons of water per minute. "One of Century City's most striking features is its architecture. There is a compelling cleanliness about Century City. More than sixty percent of Century City remains open—a strong architectural statement." (Source: Century City Chamber of Commerce, promotion material).

left: Site after clearance in 1958
right: Site plan

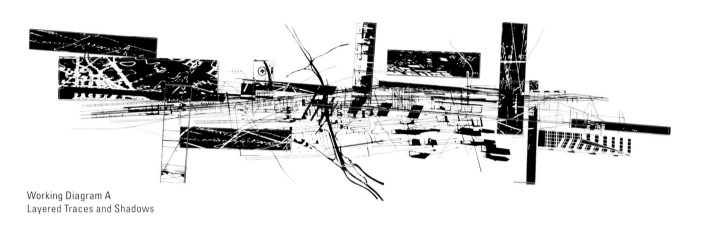

Working Diagram A
Layered Traces and Shadows

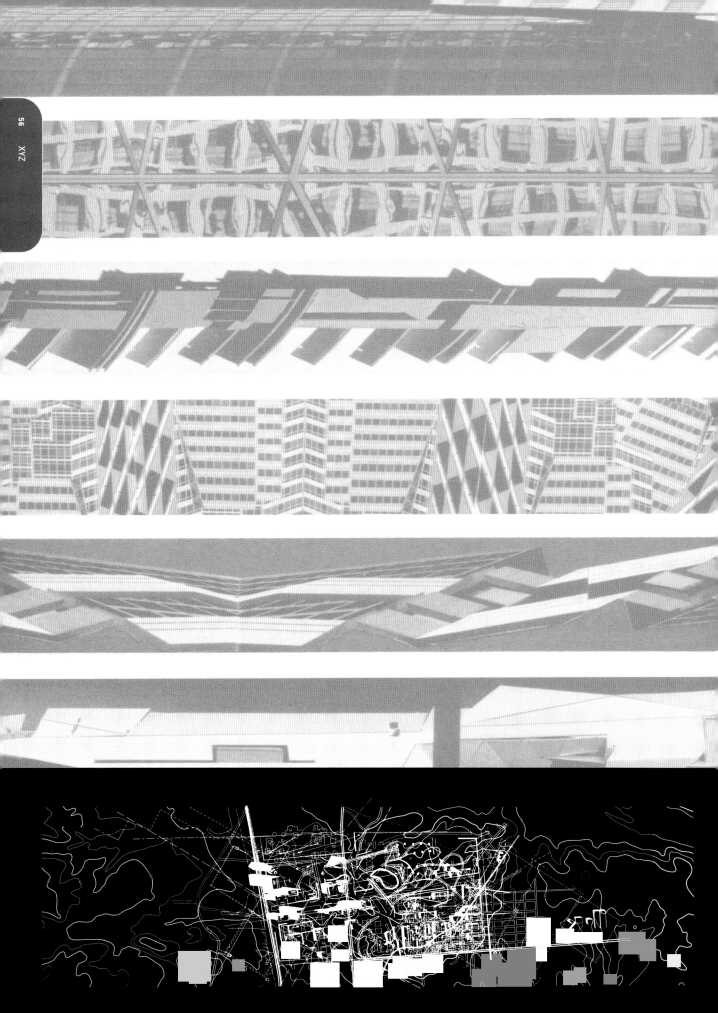

Century City proved an interesting text: a sleek, mirrored, antiseptic, and anonymous structure that hid the rather haphazard, tawdry, artificial, and vulgar nature of its previous existence as a film set. We developed a process that employed three methods of reading the site, one historical and two contemporary.

To activate Century City's past, we collected and overlaid maps of various dates. These contained the traces and markings of forgotten landscapes; dislocated film towns, movable lakes, film production sheds, oil fields, bungalow structures, and orange groves once again rose to the surface. From these residues we elaborated a new topography of traces that incorporated the previously hidden ones that had been bulldozed by the developers.[5]

We then employed three recording methods to engage Century City's present. First, shadows of the site—uncanny, transformed traces of the object of study—were recorded at different times of day and rates of motion to reflect the experience of place as perceived while driving. The shadows manifested a hidden order, an axonometric collapse of the vertical object onto a horizontal projection screen. Second, a collection of map representations were collapsed onto the shadow map.[6] Third, a filmic analysis of the site's image was employed. The sleek skins of skyscrapers dominating the site were photographed and enlarged to expose the folding and layering in the construction of their apparently smooth and uniform surfaces.[7]

Throughout this process, the resultant material was recirculated daily among the different authors for reinterpretation. We then attempted to divide the fragments we produced into two architectural categories: spatial boundaries and elements of infrastructure.

5 See map to left of collected traces (overlapping the found traces and collapsing them into one layered image) combined with a drawing of shadows of buildings and elevators projected to the ground (the shadows have been stretched in the direction of car travel).
6 See Working Diagram A on site ordering systems: Layered Traces and Shadows
7 See photograph on page 56 of Century City's skins and boundaries that have been collected and collaged.

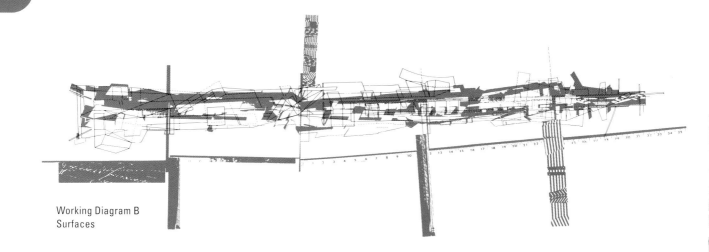

Working Diagram B
Surfaces

Century City site

8 "I think we should put some mountains here. /
Otherwise what are the characters going to
fall off of?" Laurie Anderson, *Big Science*
(Warner Brothers, 1982).
9 See Working Diagram B: Surfaces
10 As we worked on this project one of the more
interesting discussions revolved around our
understanding of Gottfried Semper, a discussion triggered by Marc Wigley at the "Sexu-
ality and Space" conference at Princeton in
1988. In his book *Der Stil in den Technischen
und Tektonischen Künsten, oder Praktische
Ästhetik* (vol. I, Frankfurt: Verlag für Kunst und

The use of veneer in this project is ultimately tied to the site's history: as a ground for filmmaking, with the conceptual purpose of providing a surface on which characters perform and do not "fall off of."[8] We used a method that is filmic, not in the conventional sense of cutting and splicing, but in its inherent structural logic. It enabled the development of space solely for the purposes of visual pleasure and as a substrate for human activity.[9] This focus on surface continued from the West Coast Gateway Competition. In the drawings and models, the simulation of pure space in an electronic and cinematic era takes priority over the traditional architectural logic of construction and the authentic representation of materials.[10]

Construction operates as an independent element in this reading, created only within the second set of working drawings, where we attempted to read an order of structure and infrastructure onto the site. Structure functions as the scaffolding that holds the skins and spatial boundaries in place. But here, the notion of pure structure is indeed called into question: it develops an existence of its own, beyond the exclusive task of "holding up." "Structure" and "infrastructure" are used here as independent but generic and formal elements with their own representational roles.

Wissenschaft, 1960), Semper offered a new and rather peculiar view of the roots of architecture. In the chapter, "The Principles of Clothing [Bekleidung] in the Art of Building," he discusses the beginnings of shelter and ornament in both primitive and sophisticated cultures such as Egypt and ancient Greece. On one hand he praises classical Greek architecture and its then recently discovered use of color for its integration of building material and surface treatment. On the other hand, he criticizes the same Greeks as having a "barbaric building culture," arguing that the "barbaric" elements of architecture—structure and ornament—are connected in a way that is inorganic, or merely mechanical and material. "It is certain that the beginning of architecture [Bauen] coincides with the beginning of textile art [Textrin]" (page 213, my translation). He insists, in contrast to Antoine Laugier and Quartremére de Quincy, that the first structures were made of woven branches, further developed woven textile elements that simultaneously supplied shelter and ornament. "The scaffolding, which serves to hold, fix, and carry these spatial boundaries [the veneer], are mere necessities that in a direct sense have nothing to do with space and spatial boundaries. They are alien to the fundamental architectonic idea and are at first not an element that defines space." (page 214) Semper points out that in the German language many words for building elements are derived from origins in textiles. For example: "Decke" means blanket as well as ceiling, and "Wand," meaning "wall," is derived from "Gewandt, or 'clothing."

As in film sets, and more recent architectural sections, the importance of the in-between space—the space of fasteners, insulation, air buffer zones, and second structures, space normally marginalized as not "space" but "technical necessity"—is revealed. Within our attempt to question established hierarchies, these in-between spaces are treated in the same way as the collected surfaces; section drawings of the surrounding generic skyscrapers were collected and distilled for structural rhythms and compositions of boundary conditions.

Transforming the vertical to the horizontal undermined the singular purpose of structure as simply "holding up." Instead, it allowed repetitive elements to "hold up" in other ways: socially, aesthetically, and structurally. They support a linear infrastructure derived from a study of the role of the elevator in Century City's skyscrapers. Forms appropriated from the freeways and train tracks describe horizontal layers, which were then translated into bicycle paths, running tracks, magnetic railways, and "x-calators"—escalators moving in cross or diagonal directions. We used working drawings as texts to further develop working models to study structures and infrastructures.[12]

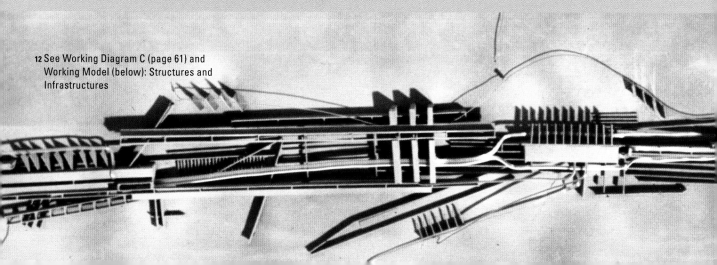

12 See Working Diagram C (page 61) and
   Working Model (below): Structures and
   Infrastructures

Working Diagram C
Structures and Infrastructures

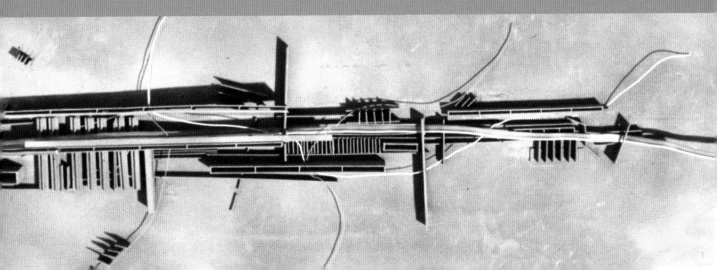

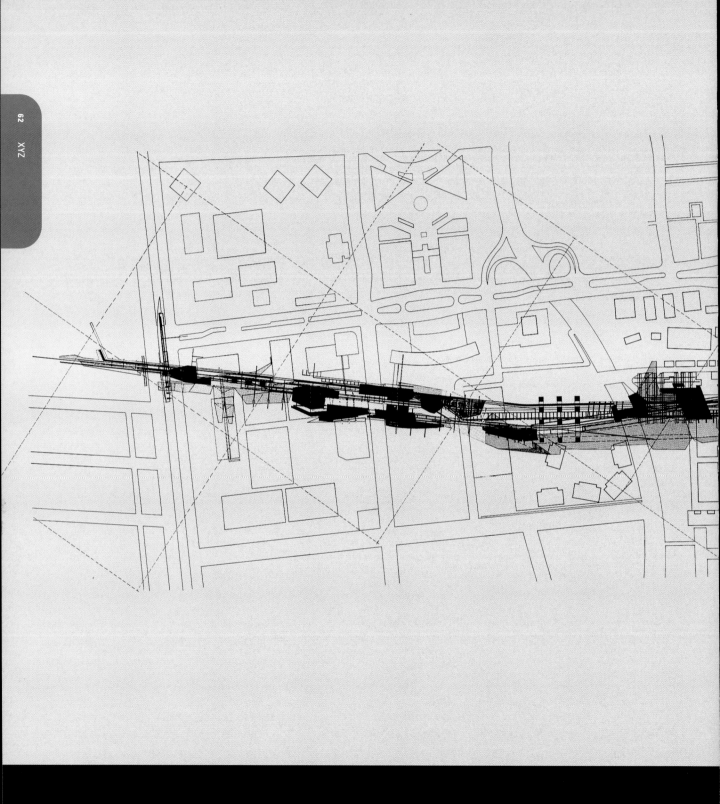

Surface Plan Diagram of Earth-Scratcher for
Century City

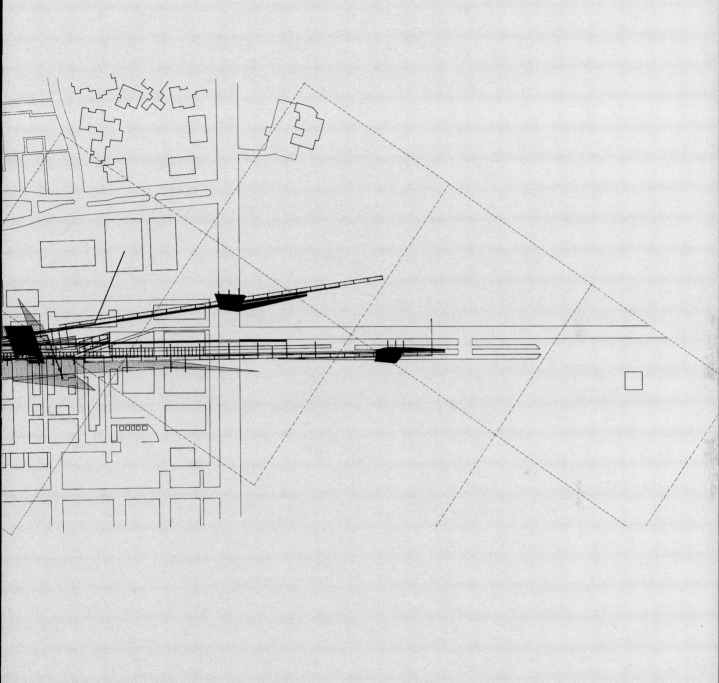

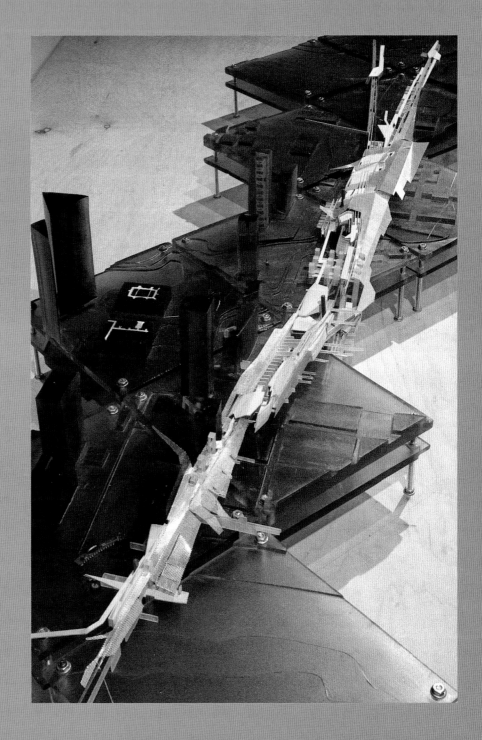

In the next stage, the collapse of these working models and drawings produced yet another model, which laid itself over Century City as an architectural parasite living off the "cleanliness" and "open space" of the office development. An earth-scratcher, it connects two different green spaces through a set of anti-programs and artificial landscapes in the form of numerous lines, surfaces, and volumes that connect, carry, and shelter human activities. The model stands as yet another text for subsequent interpretation, for further spatial development for Century City, and for the investigation of spaces at a larger scale. In fact, as a final exercise, the design team cut, spliced, copied, and layered the project's representation in order to reread the first outcome. It was then exhibited at the Royal Academy of Arts in London.

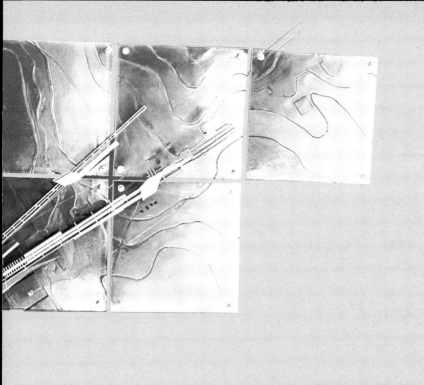

1 PRODUCED IN 1990
Principal: Dagmar Richter
Assistants: Anna Bolneset,
Joshua Levine, Cordell
Steinmetz, Robert Thibodeau,
and Theodore Zoumboulakis

2 "A feminine text cannot fail to be more than
subversive. It is volcanic; as it is written it
brings about an upheaval of the old property
crust, carrier of masculine investments;
there's no other way. There's no room for her if
she's not a he. If she's a her-she, it's in order
to smash everything, to shatter the framework
of institutions, to blow up the law, to break up
the 'truth' with laughter." Hélène Cixous, "The
Laugh of Medusa," in Elaine Marks and Isabelle de Courtivron, ed., *New French Feminism*

3 This comment was used by Stan Allen to
describe Daniel Libeskind's project for the
extension to the Berlin Museum with the
Jewish Museum Department, see Stanley
Allen, "Libeskind's Practice of Laughter: An
Introduction by Stanley Allen," *Assemblage* 12
(August 1990), 20.

THE PRACTICE OF LAUGHTER

BEING DEADLY SERIOUS

"If she's a her-she, it's in order to smash everything, to shatter the framework of institutions, to blow up the law, to break up the 'truth' with laughter."[2]

This project can be seen as an eruption in "hysterical laughter at the absurdity of reason itself."[3] In order to develop a critical architectural strategy of repair for the city of Beirut, we engaged in a practice of irony.

Numerous maps of Beirut, ranging from antiquity to the fairly recent ruins of French planning, identify successive layers of sequential catastrophe and reconstruction. We collected these maps for the express purpose of "misreading" them. Catastrophe brought about by human violence or natural disaster formed a suppressed underlay in the production of new architecture in Beirut. The architects of reconstruction have historically chosen to ignore the fact of

Beirut after the war

repetitive tragedy and instead attempted to portray a new image of undisturbed unity and timelessness. In the face of the rapid, continuous flux of
decentralized destruction and repair, architectural reconstruction and its very
capacity of representing timelessness must be radically reconsidered.

War in Beirut created a "Green Line," an impassable corridor between the
Place d'Étoile and the Place des Canons in the center of the city, where the
conflict had started. For many years, this Green Line demarcated two halves of
the city. The new Lebanese government planning agencies argued that decentralized ownership hindered the redevelopment of the existing area. They proposed to divest the original owners of their individual properties in order to
offer large-scale projects to developers.

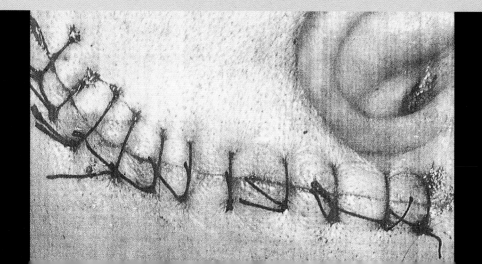

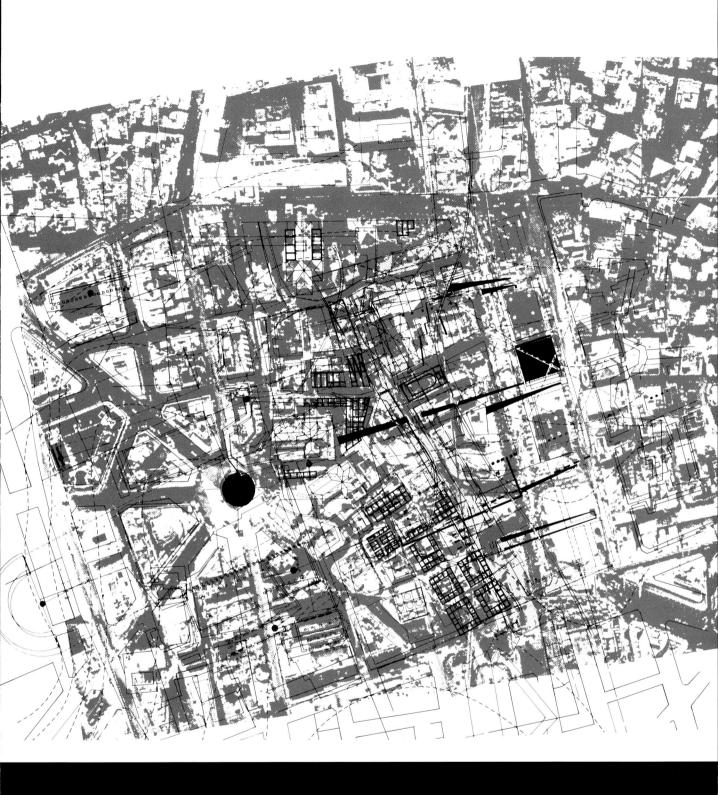

4 As a field nurse during the Crimean War, Florence Nightingale began a personal crusade to improve medical treatment in military hospitals. The nursing profession was in fact instituted as a direct response to war. Nightingale (in certain aspects) thus inspires a critical feminist position in this project: the formulation of the nurse-architect personae. We exploited systems of representation common to both soldier and nurse in developing architectural techniques of "strategy" and "operation."

Against the government plan, we chose a different strategy to reveal layers of catastrophe, leaving the old operations intact while proposing new structures. We attempted to understand the history of the city's formal changes as sectional and simultaneous; any new development would be part of this long history of layered change. We asked the government to have the courage to leave scarred areas intact and assist in a decentralized redevelopment plan through the addition of new layers.

Footnote Project: Curtain and Wall House
While developing this urban design proposal for Beirut, we had a small renovation project on the boards. For the Curtain and Wall House, a client in Westwood wanted to double the square footage of her building. A significant cultural subtext was found; the previous owner was the production designer for the film classic *Ben Hur*. The original house, where the allegorical patterns of the film world were applied to the building's interior, was left largely untouched. A new layer was created in the form of a simulated landscape

a wrapper visible from surrounding high-rise structures. Emanating from the building's existing openings, a filmic set of planes or stages for action float partly on steel shelves. Twisting, folding, slicing, and wrapping tightly around these "spaces of action" is a translucent scrim, an artificial visual landscape in the form of a curtain. This strategy of developing a two-way common visual landscape seeks to develop a new and symbiotic relationship between the disparate scales of the owner's building and its high-rise neighbors. We regarded this project as a detail of the larger

urban structures in our alternative Beirut.
Project Credits:
Produced in 1991
Principal: Dagmar Richter
Assistants: Hagy Belzberg, Eileen Yankowsky and Theodore Zoumboulakis
Engineer: Mike Ischler

As a generative device, we performed a deliberate misreading of two seemingly unrelated operations: conventional warfare and medicine. The latter, as embodied in the profession of the nurse, actually became institutionalized in response to military developments.[4] We first overlaid the markets with military maps, showing strategies of attack and counterattack. Our new representation created fields of tension and relief. Next, we used photographs of actual surgical operations on victims of war, where skin had been relocated over burns, and wounds were cleaned and sutured together. These "strategies" and "operations" became aggressive architectural tactics for inserting new structures into the destroyed area.

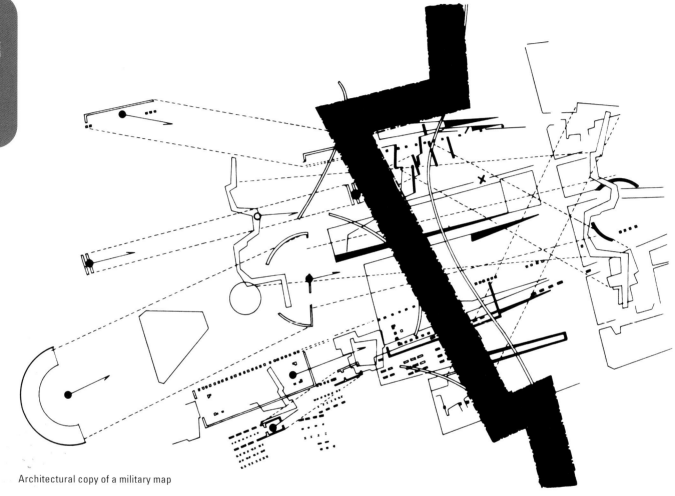

Architectural copy of a military map

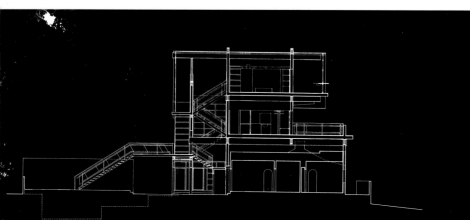

Curtain and Wall House
left: Section
right: Elevation

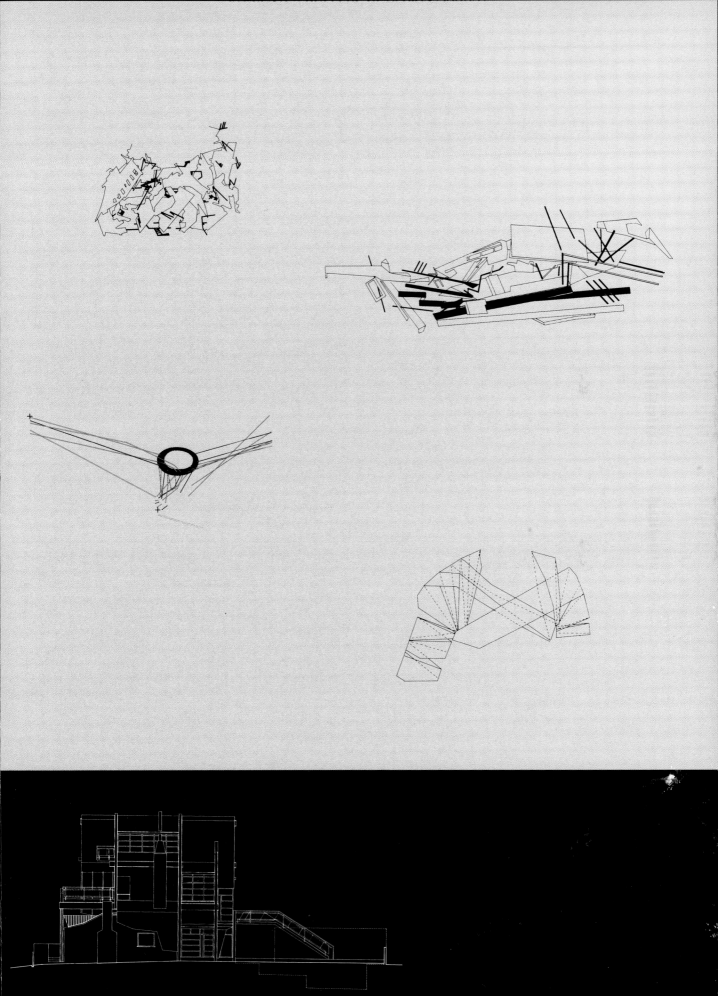

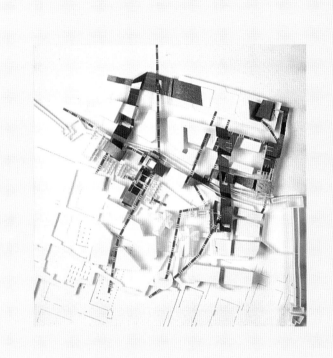

We developed an architectural veneer above and around the destroyed buildings with additional programs, which we hoped would encourage new growth
in the in-between spaces. The collective sale of air rights above these neighborhoods would maintain their partitioned and decentralized character and
inject financial benefits for initiating their own recovery. Thin threads of
pedestrian bridges created a new three-dimensional urban network, which
together with the veneer bandages reconnected the gap left by the Green Line.
The new, whimsical suture-like structures originated around the Place d'Étoile
and hovered above and between the old ruins, while new bandage veneer territories, originating at the Place Des Canons, were created by folding and
unfolding the earth's surface.

Through this aggressive insertion of new material, it became possible to repair
and transform the existing souk area without destroying its essence. Simultaneous layers of symbiotic structures confounded the city's "complete recovery" to a military state of undisturbed well-oiled visual clarity and control. Our
tactical redefinition of the highly traditional, engendered, architectural profession with military overtones as nurse-architect, developed during our practice
of laughter, changed perceived hierarchies regarding our political and cultural
role in contemporary society.[5]

5 This project was sent on to Boston and Beirut
in the form of a book.

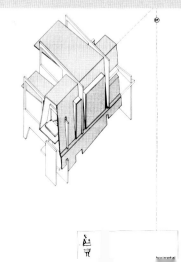
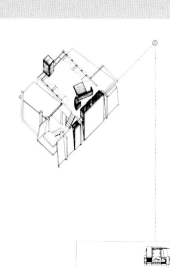

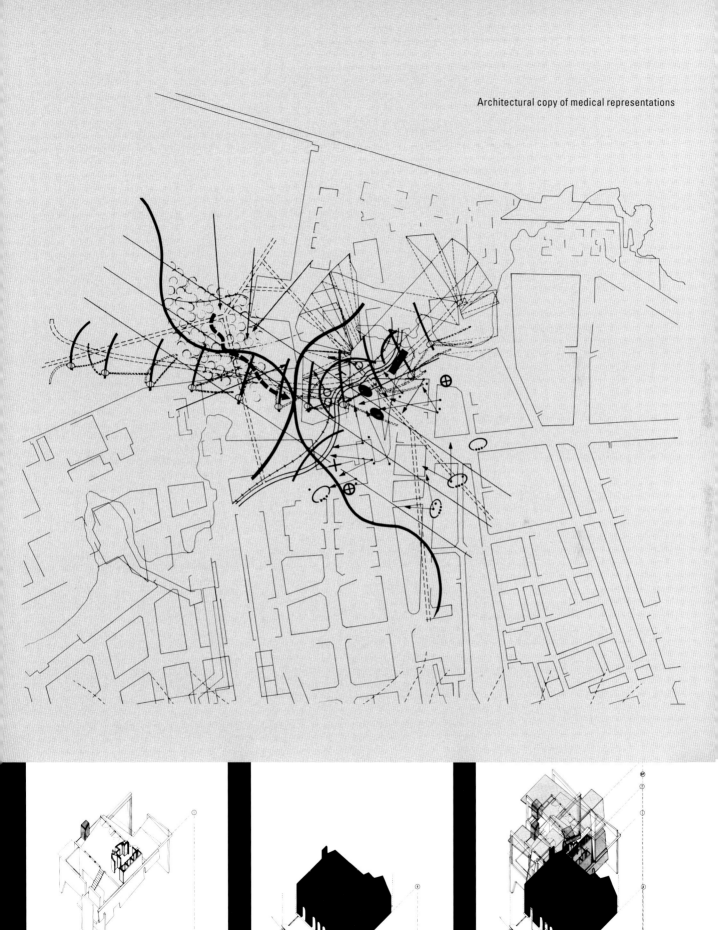

1 PRODUCED IN 1992
Principal: Dagmar Richter
Assistants: Joe Day, Nina Lesser, Jonathan Massey, Carola Sapper, and Patrick Tighe

MAPPING AS A MEANS TO AUTHORIZE

Upon reunification, Germany chose once again to bestow the title of national capital on the city of Berlin. As a result, ideas had to be generated for the integration of a new government megastructure into the western periphery of the city center. The site in question bore few traces of the series of constructions and respective destructions affected through ideologically driven planning schemes, war, and the ultimate division between East and West Germany. Instead, only weeds and ashes covered the Spreebogen site, a large void in the center of Berlin.

By first collecting different maps of this site, we initiated an investigation rooted in a political interpretation of Berlin's spatial representations, where maps mirrored political power. This process of collection, discrimination, and modification critically interpreted the site's history, as mapped by distinct, prevalent, successive, and simultaneous political and cultural concepts of order. We obtained a wide range of information, from the 1748 maps published under Count von Schmetterlich to those furnished by the competition organizers in 1989.[2] This particular site's history demanded a critical reaction. Our process of

2 The drawings of found maps—depicting the reorganization of Berlin after rationalism, Speer's plan for fascist Berlin, and the erased city structure after the Second World War—were re-represented at the studio before the design process began.

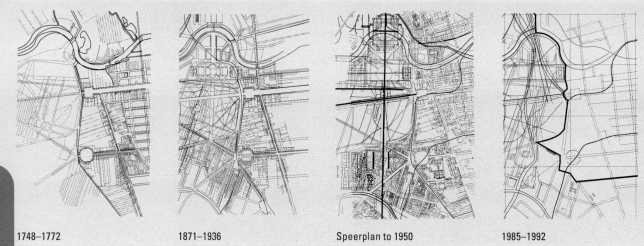

1748–1772   1871–1936   Speerplan to 1950   1985–1992

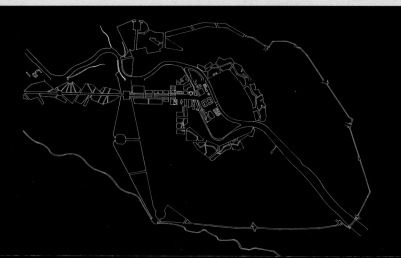

Map depicting Berlin in the fourteenth century and in the nineteenth century where
the borders were negotiated through walls
and voids

Interpretative models on the different layers
of Berlin's history made by a group of UCLA
students during a research studio

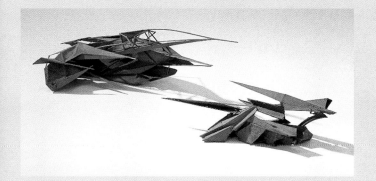

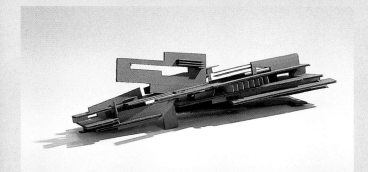

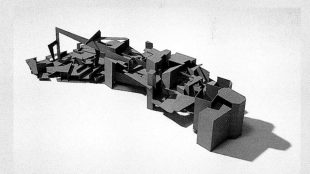

Map studies collapsed

Diagram of political force fields

formal transformation of the signs latent in these maps sought to create a space that represented democracy as a layered, diverse, and flexible system.

The depicted orders reflect clearly different prevalent, successive, and simultaneous political and cultural concepts of order throughout recent history. For example, different edge definitions reflect a permanent transformation from a certain openness for change and external influence to an order of total paranoia, which at the time of the Spreebogen competition had resulted in an immense urban wasteland.

With political and cultural goals in mind, we re-represented the maps constructively. Signs were eliminated, combined, and abstracted. From indiscriminate overlays, we distilled straight lines, curves and bubbles, organizing fields, open membranes, and closed boundaries as major formal strategies. An interpretation of the new map generated a three-dimensional model through a process of spatial weaving.

To impose new development in an area disturbed by the natural occurrence of the Spree River and the decentralized ownership of land, a north-south grid was originally applied to this site in the eighteenth century, when Berlin copied French rationalist planning models. We proposed a distribution of formally repetitive new government buildings over this same grid, fragmenting its logic and suggesting floating objects in an abstract landscape. A swarm of short parallel lines, broken off by the axes of power implemented by the Prussian nobility and Hitler's architect Albert Speer after them, ordered our proposal.

The first swarms of linear connectors are then augmented by "stitchings" in the form of long stretched curves derived from the varied path of the Spree River and the former English garden structures on the found maps. These elements negotiate and connect the Parliament, special urban events, surrounding neighborhoods, and everyday movements in the city, forming new compressed linear dynamic vectors between the Parliament, the Mitte and Friedrichstadt to the east, the workers quarters to the west, and the cultural forum to the north. This formal move was chosen in order to overcome the engineers' idea of a symmetrical and controlled river, reflecting their concept of nature versus culture. The different weavings also countered Speer's idea of a unified strict symmetrical river to fit his north-south axis. The river became a public space beyond a space of representation.

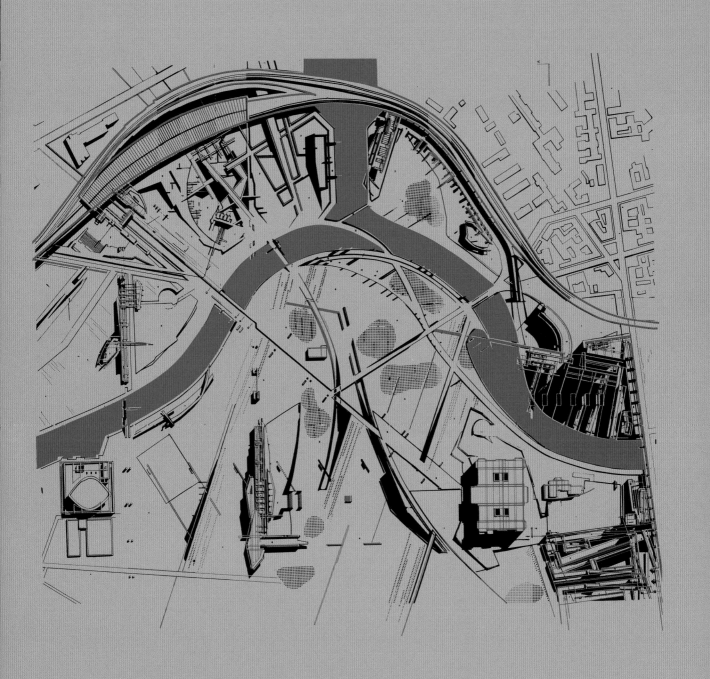

Closed borders, or unnegotiable boundaries, erected as vertical walls were found throughout the maps in single or multiple thicknesses. They were built around Berlin for military purposes in the early eighteenth century, and within Berlin to divide East and West in the mid-twentieth century. In the city, open borders, or negotiable boundaries, were then developed as voids; three squares—Pariser, Potsdamer, and Mehring plätze—correspond to entry gates and lie just inside the city walls. As effectively controlled permeable membranes, they allowed for a flow of food and materials, but afforded limited penetration for the rural farmers, thereby avoiding unpleasant class conflicts.

This found juxtaposition of solid and void influenced our proposal to fill the former Friedrichstadt area with a dense field of offices. This solid mass defined an intense edge condition to the open area of the Tiergarten, and was made negotiable through a reverse operation of erasure and dragging. Additional voids, similar to Pariser and Potsdamer plätze, were cut along this dense edge to stimulate an interpenetration of government offices and daily life. At our new Reichstag Piazza, we redefined the small existing palace adjacent to the Reichstag as a museum for German history to encourage public debate. We used another void, behind the party wing at the northern edge of the site, to interweave party members and commercial activities.

Reichstag

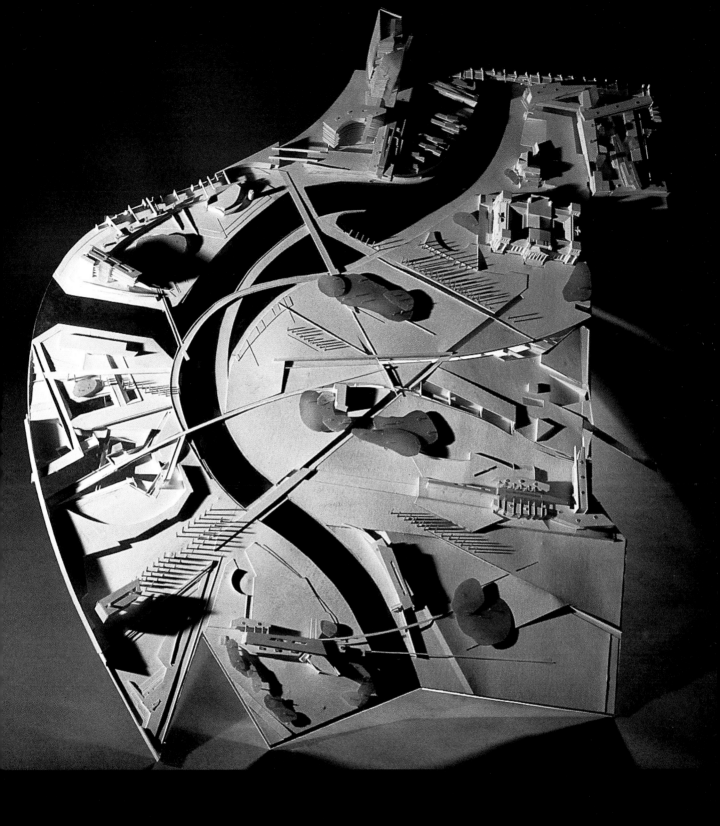

Throughout the plan we distributed fields, cityscapes, and cuts to deliver a view of the lower infrastructure to the surface. Fields of natural plantings and nodes of birch forest created "unreasonable oases" as countermeasures to an overtly predictable order. These formal "breaks" were translated from the former maps, where cartographers once attempted to represent found site conditions.

A dynamic flow diagonally connected the Cultural Forum and the Brandenburg Gate to a new multilevel rail and subway hub at Lehrter Station to the northwest. In this "river" all movement was merged and redirected, becoming a partner to the Spree in its constant flux.

Through a technique of folding, these found and transformed orders resulted in a new abstract urban landscape, where each government structure closely related to specific views and events in the city. In its undulation, it simultaneously provided panoramic views, underground parking, storage archives, and secure boundaries for sensitive government offices. Through the plane's tilt, wrapping the Reichstag, it also undermined the dominance of the Parliament building by absorbing its monumental base.

In the resulting competition proposal, different spatial orders overlapped and existed simultaneously, but did not search for a reductive and highly edited answer with artificial clarity, cultural simplicity, or a reflection of stasis, timelessness, and authoritarian comfort. Instead, the new structure always encompassed simultaneous realities and thus always included the identities of local culture and commerce, the nation as democratic, and the world connected in an information age.

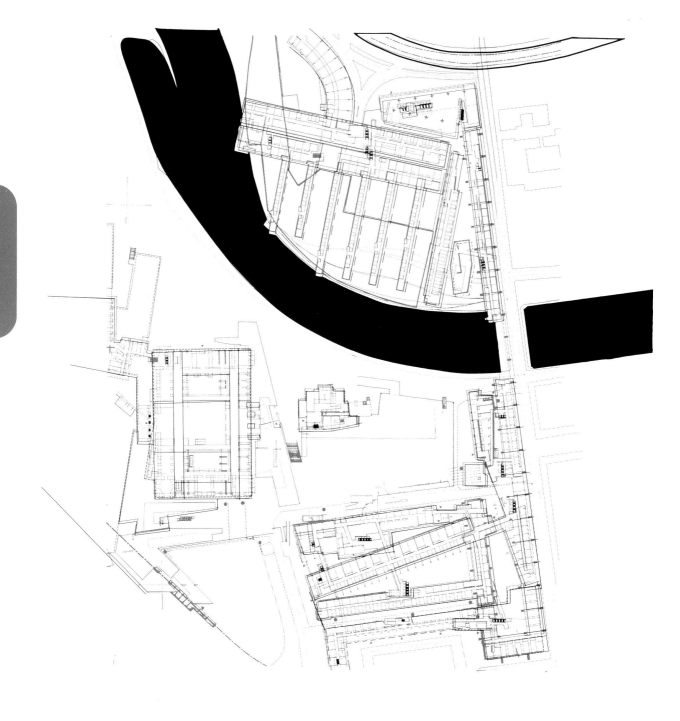

Proposed plan of government offices

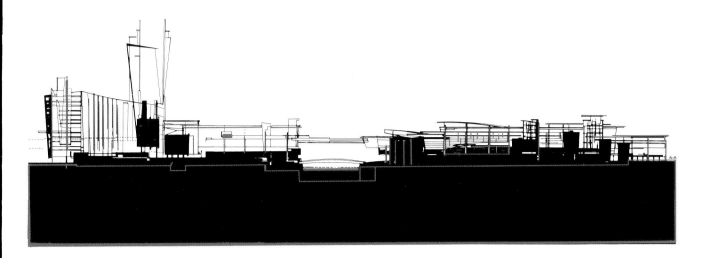

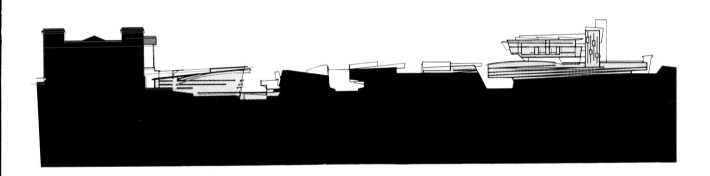

Proposed sections through government offices

1 PRODUCED IN 1993
Principal: Dagmar Richter
Assistants: N. Capelli,
M. de la Garza, L. Hansen,
C. Hampson, M. Kim, S. Oliver,
and K. Sidley

2 Rosalind E. Krauss, *The Originality of the Avant-Garde and Other Modern Myths* (Cambridge, Mass: MIT Press, fifth edition, 1988), 125.

THE ART OF COPY

"The pattern books that are the backbone of architectural production, so that a building can be cooked up from a detail taken from here and a ground plan drawn from there, are just one example of the extent to which production has always been at one level the art of making copies from other art."[2]

The following project was used to establish a methodology based on the art of copy. Most of the spaces we experience are random and circumstantial, some of them consciously formulated, most a product of chance. Daily, we are confronted with numerous levels and layers of visual text and physical experience, few of which are produced through any conscious architectural act. The reading of such texts manifests itself through the act of representing representations, of copying found material. This phenomenon is employed here to shed light on new possibilities for a critical understanding of contemporary space and the use of copying. This study is not intended to define a new style, but to further examine a methodology for the creation of form in a time when historical precedent can no longer be used uncritically.

To copy in an architectural design process is an act of unconscious appropriation that goes on continually at nearly any designer's desk. Today's "pattern books" are not the catalogs of the last century to which Krauss refers, but the magazines and journals that supply us weekly with new "patterns" ready for common consumption. In academia, a found text is normally used in quotation marks to serve an argument. The text is then transformed and commented upon to help convey the thesis in question. The architect, on the other hand, plays the game of the fiction writer, concealing and transforming appropriated texts to strengthen the myth of authorship and of the work as an authentic, original act. This myth provides the author with personal power, which can then be strategically used to promote his right to suppress other views as irrelevant. In the competition for the Royal Library of Copenhagen, this unconscious act of copy has been changed into a very conscious methodology. The planimetric and elevational information and historical material we obtained was directly copied out of the competition brief. The two-dimensional drawings were then digitized by a computerized copy machine and transformed to fit the given site.

The brief asked for a doubling of the Royal Library at the waterfront in the center of Copenhagen. In addition it asked to integrate the library into the inner city and to reorganize a mile-long stretch along the waterfront.

The Royal Library's role as a conveyor of knowledge and information has been in a continual state of transition throughout its history. Its mission changed from a primary protector and administrator of books and objects to an institution that arranges and stores information in multiple ways for mass consumption. With the advent of desktop and web publishing, the sheer mass and diversity of pictorial and textural information has become almost inconceivable. Information is produced and distributed in a more democratic fashion, as access to media becomes easier.

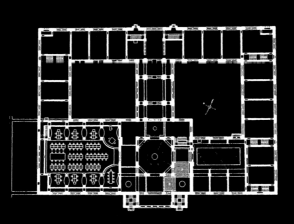

far left: Plan of found Galley House
left: Hans J. Holm's final plan of the Royal Library

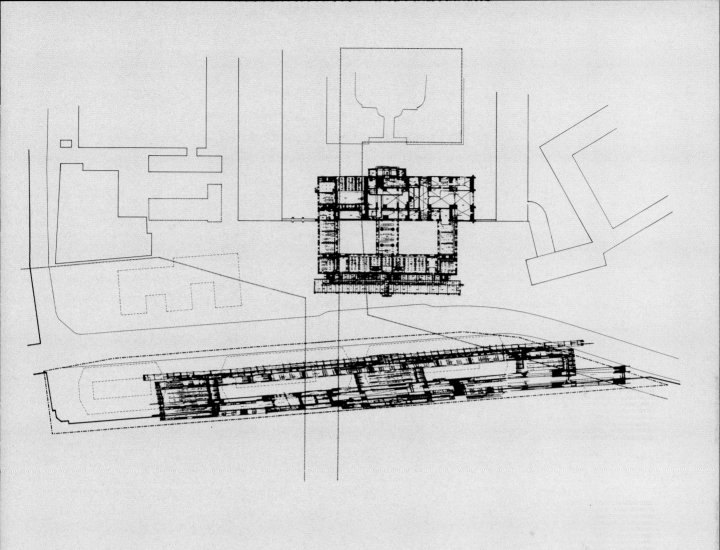

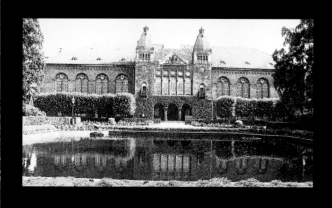

Footnote Project: Child's Guesthouse
A few years earlier we worked on a similar problem on a small scale. There we took a found object, copied and rotated its form, and expanded it through reinsertion. The found machine, a 1968 Airstream trailer, was transformed into a temporary child's guesthouse at a site in Los Angeles where zoning allowed only a carport. Sanitary facilities and the basic envelope were saved and the unnecessary parts were stripped. The child's guesthouse was designed through a confrontation of a found object and its imprints. Those imprints were rotated, copied, and relocated to create interstitial spaces between an existing "site" and wraps of architectural veneer. The resulting expansion was used for an entrance sequence, storage for toys, and a loft bed. The entire structure was bolted to a sculptured concrete platform.
Project credits:
Produced in 1989–90
Principal: Dagmar Richter
Assistants: Claudia Lueling and Joshua Levin
Engineer: Mike Ischler

Now that information may be stored electronically in minimal space, print matter will at some point in the future lose its dominance and excessive spatial requirements. Eventually, almost all information will be accessible without having to leave the home. The Royal Library will therefore take on an entirely new function, namely to collect and protect information to ensure that it remains accessible to all, and to provide a public space for discourse independent of the university.

Today we are able to read, see, or hear many diverse voices that were previously excluded from the informational stream. This development has greatly influenced architectural production. What is the best way to represent a multiplicity in the collection and arrangement of information—diversely, culturally, and architecturally—without regressing to a nonpolitical, neutral, architectural frame void of any cultural expression?

When the existing Royal Library was first planned by the architect Hans J. Holm in 1880, it was copied after a foreign model, the Royal Library in Munich, which in turn had been copied from a Florentine Renaissance palace. Holm's copy generated an "ideal" library plan heavily influenced by the beaux-arts tradition. When a site for the library was eventually chosen, the architect had to fit his ideal plan to a somewhat less-than-ideal site occupied by a rather prominent medieval building. This building, the Galley House, had to be entirely integrated into the new library, a process that quickly destroyed the autonomy of the ideal plan.

This "disturbance" inspired Holm to experiment, to a larger degree, with the possibility of culturally translating the obtained spatial information by trying to represent a newly found national Danish identity. The resultant transformation of a clean, classical building into an eclectic structure via the enforced integration of existing fabric was inspired by numerous medieval, neo-Renaissance, and eighteenth-century industrial motifs. Windows were inspired by those of

Venetian palaces, the staircase was literally copied from the Munich Royal Library, and the facade was influenced by the vernacular Danish expression of detailed brickwork. Rooms were copied from sources as disparate as French iron-framed arcades and Charlemagne's chapel in Aachen, as well as Art Nouveau sources.

This perhaps insignificant history of the beginning of the Royal Library in Copenhagen demonstrates a break from an established methodology of form-making defined by a classical vocabulary of precedence. The tension between the classical tradition and historical accuracy on the one hand, and innovation and a search for national identity on the other, surfaced even in countries like Denmark, hardly at the forefront of vanguard cultural production. Holm, a "royal architect," was either unable or unwilling to take up this intellectual challenge for critical reconsideration. Instead, he imported a potpourri of motifs from "higher" cultures: a collection of unclassified references composed his "national library." This rather unconscious and uncritical copying, translation, and transformation resulted in a pastiche of haphazardly assembled cultural fragments.

The new library was opened in 1906. The original plan was considered a half execution of a bilateral cross-plan, which later was to be mirrored in the space of the library garden, should the need arise. This library garden, however, became a very important and beloved public space in the inner city of Copenhagen and today could no longer be disturbed.

The program for the new Royal Library asked for a new space that would double its size. This change in size was read as a mirror condition—a mirror of identity—which was used in my studio as a conceptual base for further interpretations on spatial precedence.

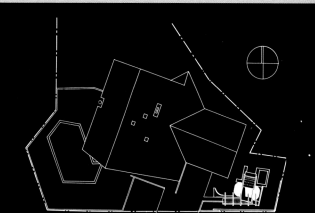

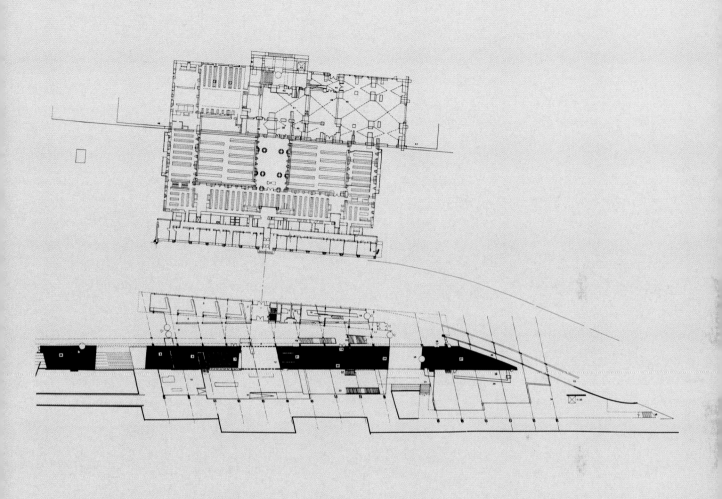

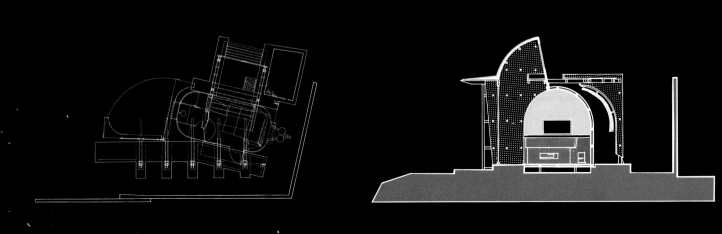

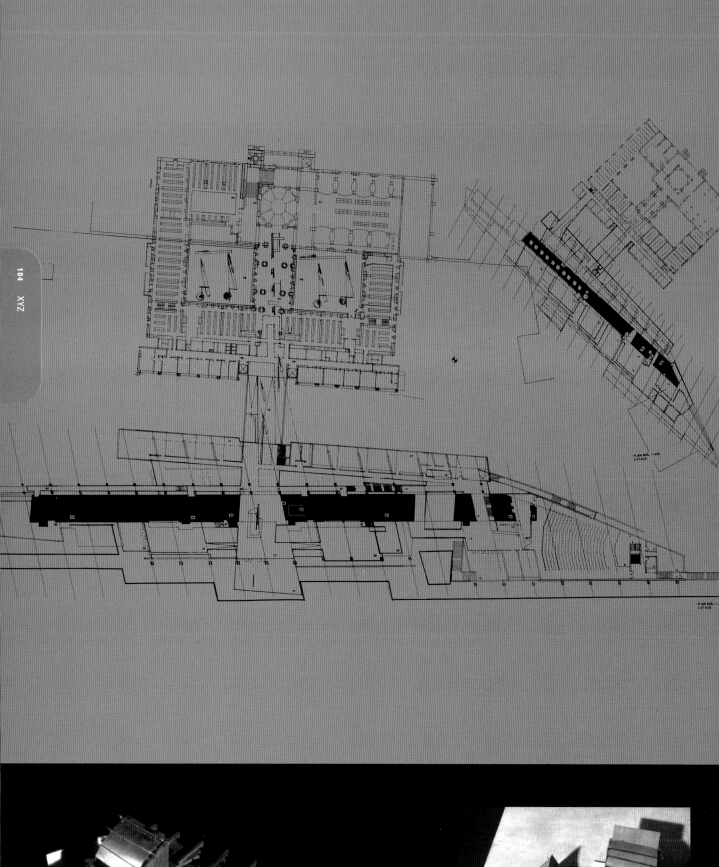

PLAN MÅL 1:400
C-ETAGE

PLAN MÅL 1:
C-ETAGE

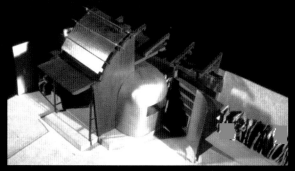

We digitized the found plan of the existing library and stretched it to the given site's proportion. Instead of using a precedent from the magazines, to help us "cook up a building by taking a detail from here and a ground plan from there"[3] we used the existing library as a found object, an identity to be recognized. The original goal of eventually mirroring the library plan into the garden to achieve the perfect beaux-arts symmetry was appropriated and diverted. It inspired us to mirror the found plan towards the water without the goal to achieve a historical but questionable beaux-arts plan.

We used contemporary circumstances, such as views to and from the city, access from surrounding activities, security, protection, programmatic needs, and our determination to create a public forum, to establish new rules. We then copied, rotated, and cut parts of the new "ideal" plan. This resultant plan generated material for programmatic and spatial interpretation that was then further translated into plan and section, creating a building with clear zones and a flexible function.

The new stretched library plan is built up in strips layered parallel to the water. The assigned programs reflect, in a mirrored fashion, what actually happened in the existing library. All zones in the new and existing library are stitched together by two volumes that cut partial voids into both buildings and carry multiple ramps connecting staggered levels.

Zone one, nearest the waterfront, contains the reading rooms that open toward the water and function as a public forum for the arrangement and distribution of information. All reading rooms are located on floating balconies within a larger volume. Direct visual contact is maintained between them, much like the balconies in a theater, only the spectacle here is the city itself.

3 Krauss, *Originality of Avant-Garde,* 125. This small paragraph actually covers a lot of material that concerns this work.

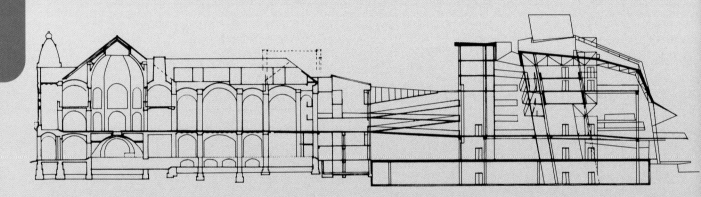

Cross section

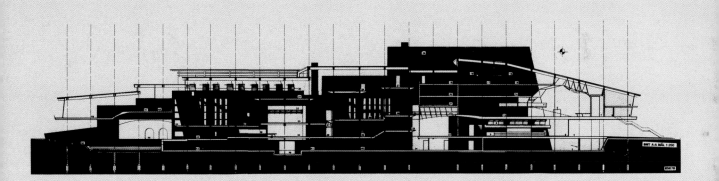

Longitudinal section

Zone two is a wall for information storage, which keeps zone one free of traffic and noise, and is formally derived from the transformation of the voids of the existing courtyards into a solid book-wall. The wall is also an organizing element where the individual user may orient herself and learn how to access information from computer terminals. All information, digital or print, is stored here in a series of containers within containers, located within the massive structure of the wall; each container can be individually closed and locked against fire, theft, and climatic dangers. The wall, physically and intellectually, "holds everything down," as its dominant presence in the elevation facing the city suggests.

Zone three is a void through which one enters the library. By slipping sideways into this large, tall space, one may then access all the ramps, stairs, and elevators that connect to exhibition halls, the library, cafeteria, concert hall, administration offices, and connected independent institutes.

Zone four house the library's administration and reflects the administration wing of the old library with the same small and repetitive partitioning. All different zones, in both the new and old buildings, are stitched together by a swarm of ramps and folded planes.

For the elevation of the new library we scanned the existing roof landscape as it is experienced from the water's edge and manipulated its form according to programmatic needs. The resulting folded plane is to be made of copper acting as a foreground to the Parliament Building and the existing library's roof. The new library copies the found formal vocabulary but achieves, through abstraction and appropriation, a new vocabulary that is able to renegotiate the dichotomy of old and new architecture.

Footnote Project: NATO Monster
During our design for the winning scheme of the Royal Library competition our team also produced a "loser" project. This project engaged in the discussion on Denmark's relationship to NATO, which at that time was quite strained. We proposed a project called "books instead of war machines." We took an existing NATO carrier stationed in Denmark, cut it open, added a new skin wrapping around the found object and docked it permanently to the given site's waterfront with bridge connections to the existing library.

Both library projects were sent to Denmark at the same time. Officially the "NATO Monster" (as we called it) project got lost and never even made it to the competition exhibition.
Project Credits:
Produced in 1993
Principal: Dagmar Richter
Assistants: Nick Capelli, Mercedes de la Garza, Liza Hansen, Carl Hampson, Marc Kim, Scott Oliver, and Keith Sidley
Model: Nick Capelli

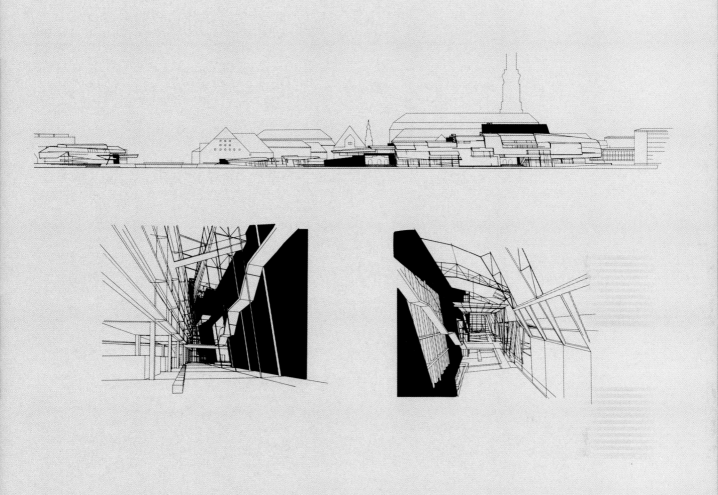

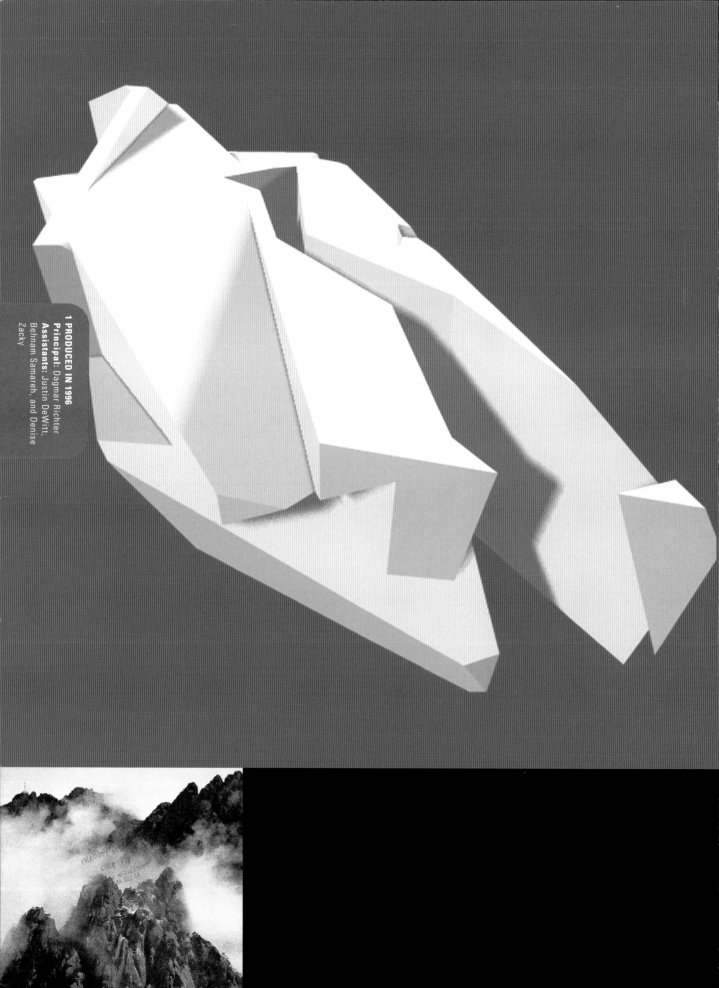

1 PRODUCED IN 1996
Principal: Dagmar Richter
Assistants: Justin DeWitt,
Behnam Samareh, and Denise
Zacky

INNER FOLDS, CURVES, AND SHIFTS

LANDSCAPES AND CULTURAL PRECEDENCE

The design process for this competition reflects our particular concern for issues of cultural heritage and precedence in non-Western cultures. The Shanghai Competition required participants to develop a new housing concept for a fictitious site on the outskirts of the city. Shanghai, like so many other contemporary Asian cities, had long abandoned opportunities to further develop and research an architectural discourse that addressed its own cultural heritage.[2] I therefore embarked upon a critical research project to spark a debate that was, until now, entirely lacking.

2 Interestingly enough, I found a recognizable Chinese copy of my own design as a "precedence" on page 8 of the competition manual. In 1982, I completed a design for a new housing project competition for the city of Regensburg, Germany for the Bornebusch office from Copenhagen. Our design won first prize. This new city has been largely constructed.

In Asian cities that had surrendered to Western prototypes, architecture was regarded as simply an art of stylistic copy. Our criticism of this fact led us to study and copy the traditional Chinese gardens as a cultural precedent. Known for highly articulated, artificially contoured surface conditions, the gardens are described as varied, contemplative, and sophisticated spatial sequences using the presence of cherished rock formations. These dramatic artificial formations, with deep crevices and folds seemingly carved by natural forces, were regarded as a high art form for thousands of years. The aim of this tradition was to increase and intensify the external surfaces of natural-looking stones in order to add visual and textural interest and richness to the garden.[3]

3 Simon Schama's book *Landscape and Memory* was very inspiring in our discourse on how to read landscape. His historic description of the first discussions in the Alpine Club in the 1830s helped form our idea of landscape as a performing surface. He describes in his book a very interesting conflict occurring between John Ruskin and Viollet le Duc. Ruskin apparently described the alpine formations as a collection of folds, curves, and shifts. But he was especially taken aback by Viollet le Duc's proposal to rhomboid or trapezoid forms. Schama writes, "The *Fragment of the Alps* is a Ruskinian manifesto. And it was meant as an attack on lazy images of geological formation, not only in respect of their brilliant color but, even more critically, in respect of their essential shape. Perhaps the greatest of all the revelations that had come to Ruskin, the one that seemed to him to signify how paramount the place of rocks was in creation, was their wariness of deep form." (Simon Schama, *Landscape and Memory* [New York: Alfred A.

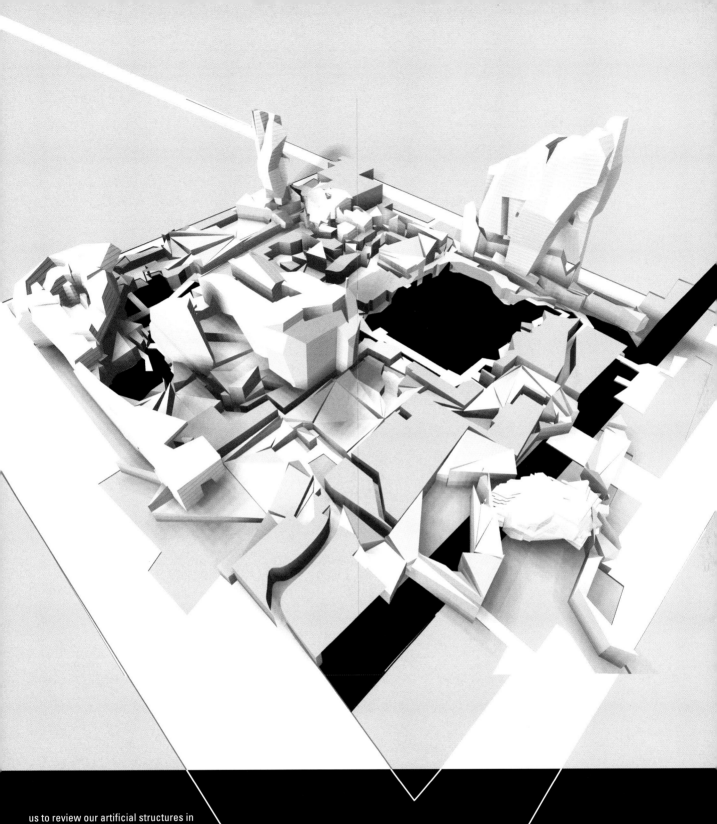

us to review our artificial structures in
their whole inner folds, curves, and shifts
and not just in terms of surface performance.

We also studied, from existing gardens, path typologies that opened views or that provided distinct and varied spatial scenarios in often-compressed spaces.[4] Dominant features of the gardens, such as artificial hill and water formations, provided the impetus for a new urban design concept as a possible alternative to the well-established Western typologies of housing design: the modernist high-rise model, and worse, the land-consuming model of American suburban expansion. Inspired by the Chinese landscape tradition, we designed our own artificial hill formation. The result was a performative folded skin that would achieve dense and, in some cases, relatively large housing volumes. Through a process of copying, overlapping, and then scanning the formal features of several significant local gardens and hill formations outside of the city,

4 See plan at right of "Net Master's Garden."

Footnote Project: Fine Arts Seismic Facility at UC Riverside
This project was produced shortly after the Shanghai 2000 project, in a complex but rather typical collaboration. The design office Israel Callas Shortridge collaborated with the two design consultants Annie Chu and myself for the design of this project (which had been worked on by the late Frank Israel in its initial stage). The given program, containing 97,000 square feet, had gone through various major revisions in the past. It contains teaching facilities and administrative and faculty areas for the university's departments of art history, dance, music, theater, and studio arts, together with a number of performance spaces and interdisciplinary facilities that will be frequented by outside visitors. Annie Chu and I realized during the design process that we both were extremely fascinated by the rock formations and designs of Chinese gardens, which resulted in a novel building-landscape relationship. The building, which has just finished construction, offers several datum-planes located at the exterior. It carries the students to many levels on folded, sculpturally shaped landscape-like platforms and from there into the interior of the different departments. It therefore weaves diverse and proportionally different spaces into a very prominent and challenging gateway site. The entire building is designed as a series of sculptural elements implying a generous kinetic flow from the fine arts mall across the very public court and stairs via balconies, low roofs, and roof tops toward a calmer and more protective back.

Project Credits:
Design Architect: Israel Callas Shortridge
Principal in Charge: Barbara Callas
Project Designer: Annie Chu
Design Consultant: Dagmar Richter
Project Architect: Thomas Stallman

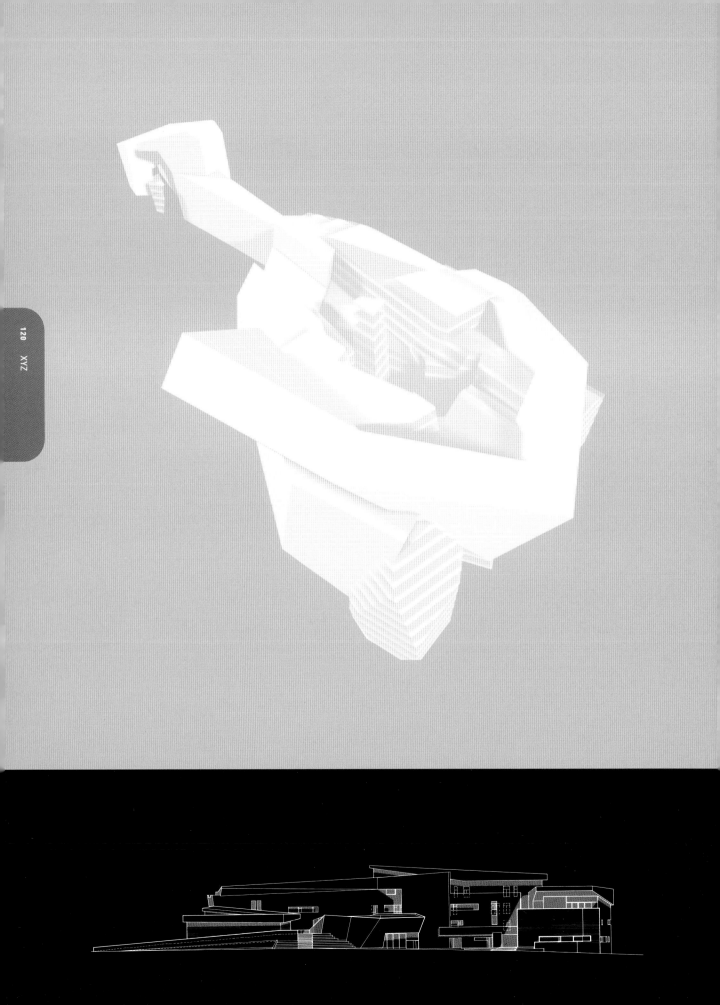

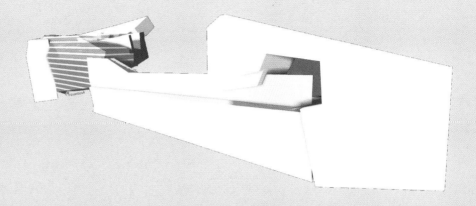

we developed a sculptural, three-dimensional computer model. Surface qualities of shifts and folds between the exterior and interior created a range of possibilities to develop more specific apartment formations. The newly achieved shapes proved suitable for carrying public infrastructure and walkways on the exterior. Denser structures at the base of the surface provided large volumes for food markets, shops, restaurants, and leisure centers. We introduced water surfaces to create voids, contemplative mirror surfaces, and airflow that intensified but did not overburden the housing complex. The Chinese garden model demonstrated the feasibility of developing a symbiotic and adaptable dense artificial landscape upon a generic and uninspiring site.

1 PRODUCED IN 1994
Principal: Dagmar Richter
Assistants: Michael Brem,
Sam Sheppert, and Gudrun
Wiedemer

PERFORMING MEMBRANES

The perceived materiality of architecture is presently in flux. It no longer relies on centuries-old definitions of firmness. Our spatial concepts have been forever altered by both the advent of the electronic age and the appearance of new materials.

My entry to the 1994 Shinkenshiku Membrane Competition, "Super-Space Working," was predicated on assumptions about the future development of space and infrastructure. Electric energy will continue to proliferate as fossil fuel usage declines. Developments in construction technology will force a shift from heavy and singular architectural typologies, such as the elements of "wall" and "column," to a new layered and complex arrangement of space through skins, membranes, and electronically controlled climatic devices. Architecture in the future will be lighter and more adaptable to functional, cultural, structural, and climatic challenges.

Site photograph

We used recent technological developments as a basis for speculation on the spatial possibilities of the near future. It is conceivable that modern industrialized nations will soon increasingly promote electric automobile usage to overcome air pollution.[2] In the transitional phase, when all roads are shared by both electric and gas-powered vehicles, existing highways are likely to be the first roads to receive attention for dramatic improvements. Conductive road surfaces have already been proposed by several electric utility companies as a solution to the problem of long distance travel in battery-powered vehicles. Existing highway infrastructure could then be reorganized into an extensive toll road system for electric vehicles only, where energy use per mile is instantly charged to credit cards. All car types would continue to share only city and rural routes, until such a time when a complete conversion to electric vehicle usage is effected.

2 Electric car with my kids

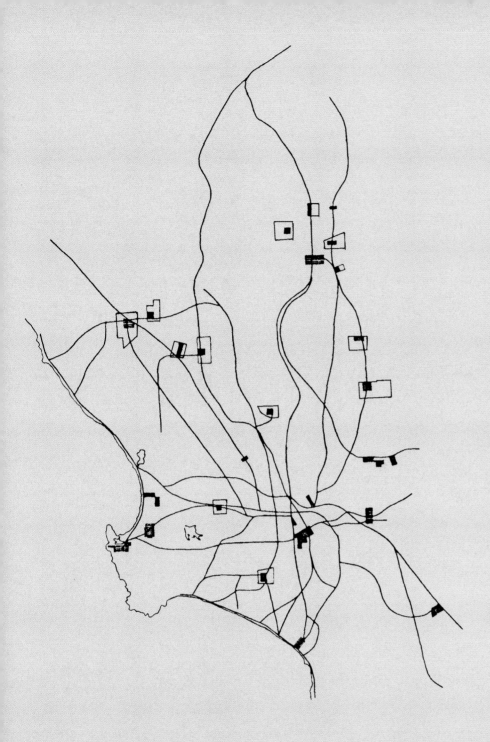

Highway development through LA's frag-
mented center

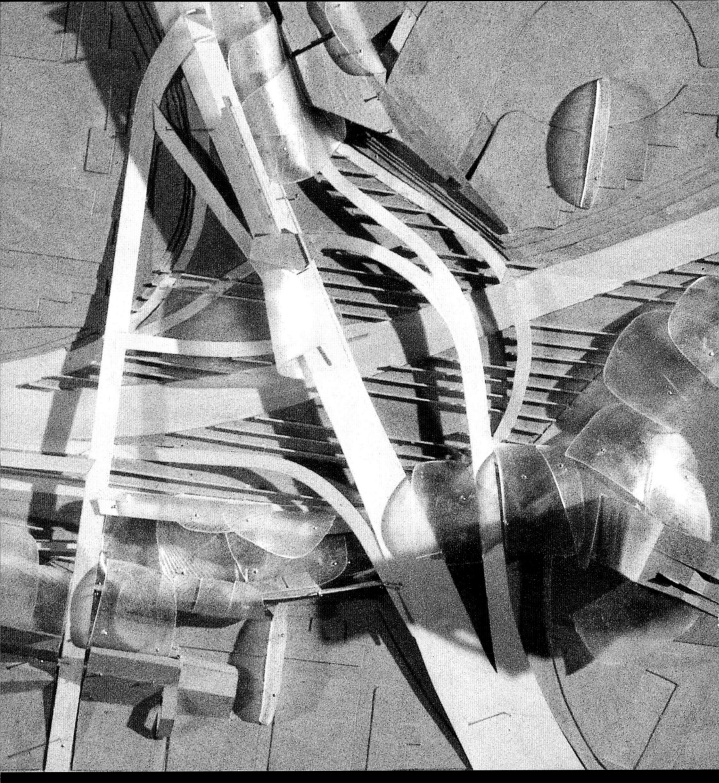

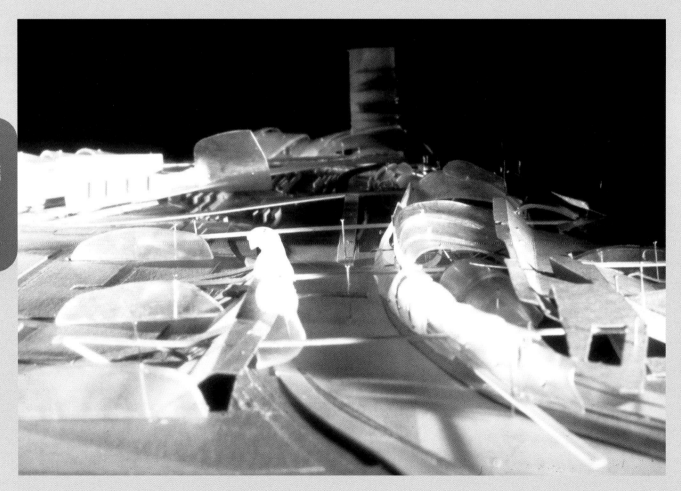

Contemporary highways cut through our neighborhoods, creating unnecessary air and noise pollution. As a result, adjacent real estate is underutilized and poorly maintained. This proposal investigates the potential of these marginal and largely abandoned spaces, which otherwise provide immediate and convenient access to transport connections. The numerous "leftover" strips of land along these urban and suburban arteries could potentially withstand extensive redevelopment into centrally located workspaces if not for the existing noise and air pollution. If these two detractions associated with the use of fossil fuels could simply be removed, highways would be as attractive as natural rivers, providing interesting views and a connection to the now nearly silent flows of urban, suburban, and interurban life.

Present and future changes in the materiality of architecture enable a reconsideration of the unimaginative and excessive land-use policies of the prevailing office-building-as-object typology. This proposal seeks to blur the distinction between object (that is, architecture as figure) and landscape (that is, void or ground for visual pleasure and infrastructure only).

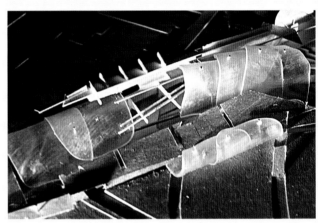

To investigate the possibilities of a new office-as-landscape typology, we intentionally combined the commercial workplace and the spaces of agricultural production in an instance of cross programming. For the purposes of climate control many large-scale agricultural products are grown in partial or completely enclosed interior conditions. Strawberries and lettuce are presently grown in commercial greenhouses or outdoor fields covered with plastic.[3] Flowers, fruit, and vegetables as well as many specialized agricultural products could conceivably begin to colonize the spaces along electric highways. Genetically altered crops will soon grow hydroculturally, eliminating the need for pesticides. These fields of production may then provide not only visual pleasure and leisure space for adjacent office workers, but also a mutually beneficial climatic arrangement.

As these new programmatic combinations and technological developments influence architectural language, materials such as titanium and fiberglass come to be used with light membranes encapsulating flexible space for the increased productivity and well being of all users. In urban contexts, these new structures reconnect old neighborhoods, bridging the previous highway divide with dense and active social spaces.

3 Plants grown in membranes

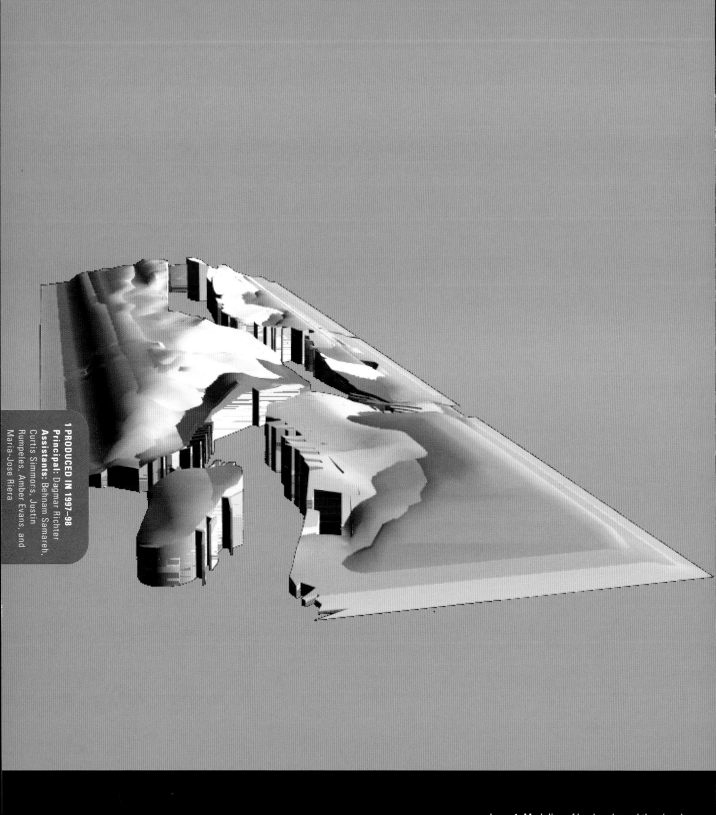

1 PRODUCED IN 1997–98
Principal: Dagmar Richter
Assistants: Behnam Samareh,
Curtis Simmons, Justin
Rumpeles, Amber Evans, and
Maria-Jose Riera

layer 1: Modeling of landmarks and the visual
voids they could create
layer 2: Modeling of large infrastructures and
their influence
layer 3: Modeling of domestic interiors translated into housing
layer 4: Modeling of public interiors translated
into institutions, offices, and retail space

DATASCAPES

By 1997, new and more sophisticated computer modeling tools enabled us to realize a project for an electronic spatial zoning map. The idea was to create a kind of pulsating digital landscape that would register the changes of society instantaneously and strategically react to the dynamics of the city as an urban organism. The creation of three-dimensional computer-animated diagrams, we believed, could generate a sophisticated and more tactical datascape to accommodate new architectural operations. We proposed a framework more sophisticated and sensitive to local developments, reactive to economic and statistical changes, and convincing as well as negotiatory in its implementation of a greater amount of public space and layers of programmatic hybrids in the city's section.

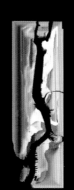

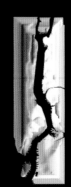

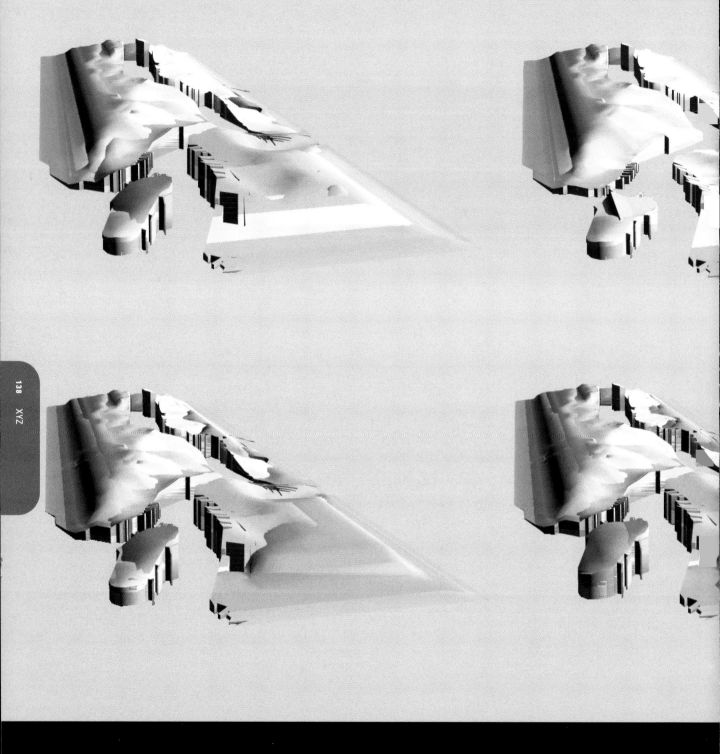

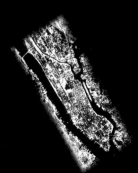

This project began in 1997 with Manhattan as its theoretical base. In the following year, we applied this model to an urban design proposal for the area between piers sixteen and eighteen on the Lower East Side of Manhattan. The Van Alen Institute, which was then conducting a design competition for redevelopment along the East River, provided spatial and statistical data for this area, which we then translated into a three-dimensional computer-animated map representing intensities.[2] Program clusters such as external public space, infrastructure, internal public space (offices), and internal private space (housing, manufacturing, government, and surveillance) were identified and modeled into a layered, three-dimensional model. This model was then animated to react to differences in the development of collected data.[3] Eventually, all of the programmatic layers were meshed together in order to react to each other's changes. The outcome was a hybrid, three-dimensional, mental, animated, programmatic sponge, where a number of activities were possible in this section of the city.

2 I was intrigued by Deleuze and Guattari's definition of a Body without Organs—a "BwO"—since it described our new reading of the city as an organism, which, in actuality, could not be master-planned in the traditional sense. "Peopling of BwO, a Metropolis that has to be managed with a whip. What peoples it, what passes across it, what does the blocking? A BwO is made in such a way that it can be occupied, populated only by intensities. Only intensities pass and circulate. Still, the BwO is not a scene, a place, or even a support upon which something comes to pass." Gilles

Deleuze and Félix Guattari, A Thousand Plateaus: Capitalism and Schizophrenia, trans. Brian Massumi (Minneapolis: University of Minnesota Press, 1987), 153.
3 In this project we were working with a new definition of form as diagram instead of formal composition. We were certainly influenced by the texts floating around in the architectural profession trying to describe control mechanisms that stay as flexible as abstract machines do. "Deleuze and Guattari developed their theory of abstract machines, engineering diagrams defining the structure

generating process that give rise to more or less permanent forms but are not unique to those forms, that is, they do not represent (as an essence does) that which defines the identity of those forms." Manuel De Landa, "Conclusions and Speculations" in A Thousand Years of Nonlinear History (New York: Swerve Editions, 1997), 263.

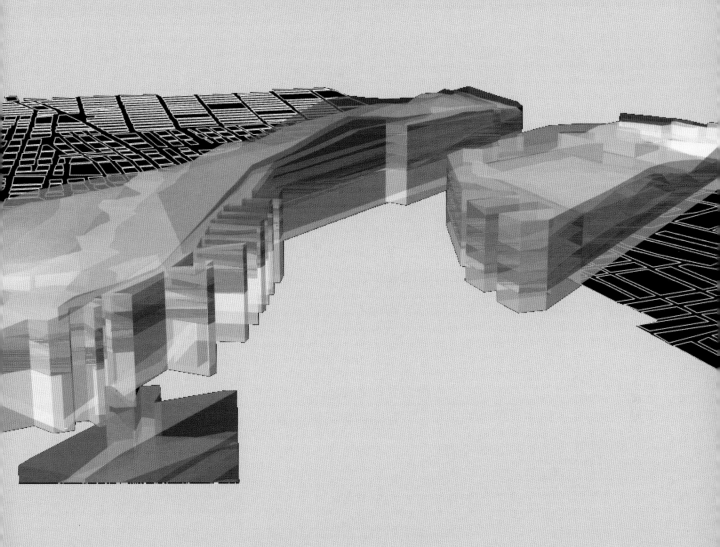

Footnote Project: A House on Top of a House
In a single-family residence in Santa Monica,
we explored the possibilities of configuring an
experimental structure within very restrictive
planning and design guidelines. While the
street facade respects the given context, the
project opens itself toward the back with an
experimental vigor. This enlivens the neigh-

across loft spaces on the upper plane. The
building cuts visually through different
spaces as well as through several buildings in
the neighborhood, thus reconfiguring the
public-private domain.
Project Credits:
Produced in 1997–98
Principal: Dagmar Richter

We then proceeded to produce a case study by taking the resulting zoning sponge around the area between piers sixteen and eighteen and playing out a new zoning scenario where a meshwork of different program types occupied the datascape. The resulting architecture, which then operated within the given framework, provided public parks at the rooftop, public programs in its lower section, and housing and workspace within its main volume. We also inserted new programs within an adjacent skyscraper. At the time of this project New York City already suffered under inflexible zoning laws; the buildings around Wall Street had a high vacancy rate, as office space was less in demand. This new zoning model could provide reprogramming and multi-programming within the section of a new as well as an existing building.

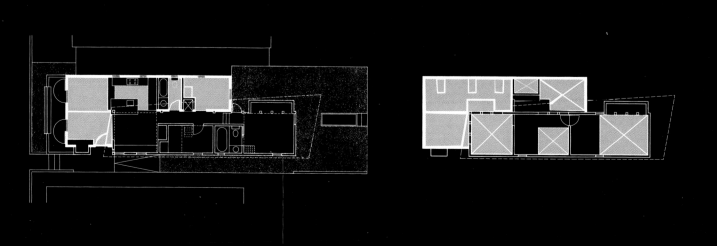

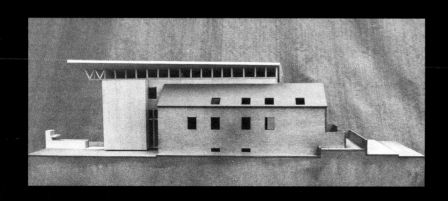

Model of case study

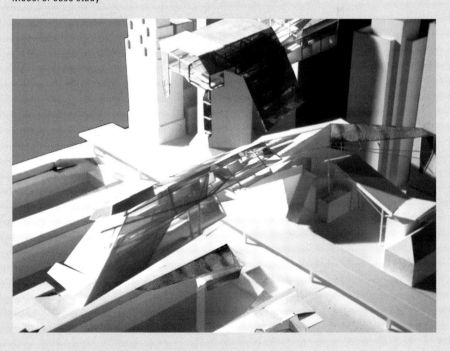

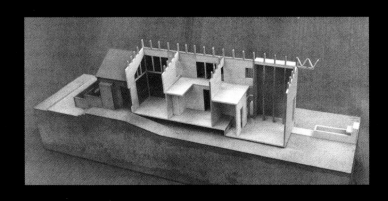

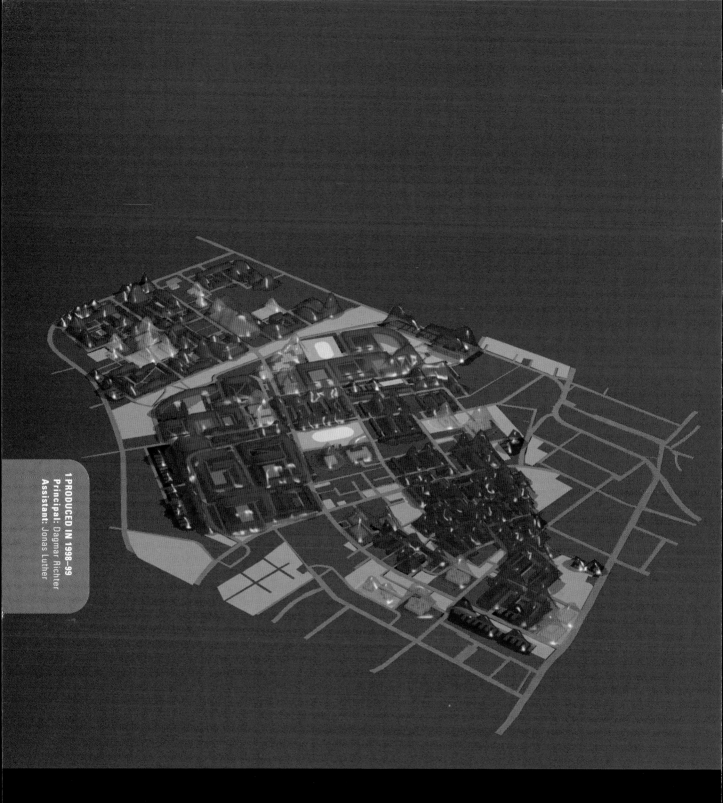

1 PRODUCED IN 1998-99
Principal: Dagmar Richter
Assistant: Jonas Luther

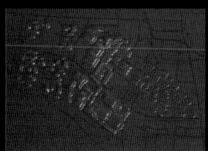

Density of inhabitants

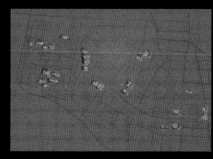

Activity level around public buildings

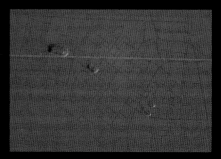

Activity level of supermarkets

MESHWORKS

URBANISM AT THE MARGINS

"But in addition to stratified, formal power, there is power of the meshwork type, that is destratified power operating via a multiplicity of informal constraints. In this book we treated these constraints as catalysts, or triggers, that play the role intercalary elements in the formation of meshworks."[2]

The most challenging text today lies in the periphery of former Eastern Block socialist city structures, where we experience a collapse of landscape, infrastructure, and city. Here, we are forced to reconsider traditional concepts of city and landscape as well as production, housing, and leisure.[3] We are forced to reconsider in particular the role of planning rationality, since found spaces are the outcome of the failed centralist planning ideology of the former socialist regimes. The collapse of many socialist structures and their own

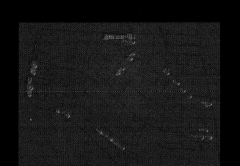

2 Manuel De Landa, *Conclusions and Speculations: A Thousand Years of Nonlinear History* (New York: Swerve Editions), 270.

reinvention in a highly dynamic capitalist structure reveals the planner's ideological crisis since his role as planner has been slowly rendered irrelevant by the blooming capitalist system.

In the former socialist East Germany we find ourselves in a postindustrial and post functional operative landscape and an agglomeration of former operative structures, which have been largely rendered irrelevant. Here the planners seem obviously powerless. Suddenly we cannot operate as traditional timeless artistic composers on a conceptually uncontaminated and neutralized site, but need to consider arbitrary and dynamic changes in a landscape, where fragmentary interventions, temporary conditions and shrinkage are prevalent.

Certainly, powerful computers and software have made it possible to process an immense mass of data in a short amount of time. We wanted to know how a more sophisticated and dynamic zoning model could create a pulsating mental landscape that would be able to register the changes of society more reactively. Here, an animated computer model of forms, as mental landscapes, would be able to create a dynamic and more adaptable framework in which architecture would operate. The model creates a structure that is more sophisticated and sensitive to local developments, reactive to economic and statistical changes, and convincing as well as negotiatory in its implementation of a greater amount of public space and hybrids of programmatic layers.

3 Project Material:
Social data: density of inhabitants—potential for engagement
Supermarkets: high-predefined consumption, low social or other action to be used as magnetic attractors for new dynamic social possibilities
Garages: low predefined consumption, high appropriation of already existing goods—used as baseline for engagement
Public buildings: used as high places for pre-given packaged information with potential for appropriation

Green space: used as potential for movement and temporal action
Infrastructural base structures: used as a base for animation programs that create loops from the base system in order to reconnect more tissue
Housing structures: used as either potential transformative voids or dense social potential dependent on the found density in the buildings

Mass-produced housing from the former socialistic government of the German Democratic Republic was our site of interest. The ideology of modernism had been taken on at face value at the southern area around Berlin in the last century. Industry had been stamped out of the formerly rather pastoral landscape around Dessau starting in the middle of the last century, when useful minerals and coal were found. The entire landscape was reorganized into an industrially productive landscape of a very different scale. Small rural towns were quickly removed when useful material was found underneath them. A new class of industrial entrepreneurs and industrial workers entered the area, producing an industrial landscape that did not grow out of the classical, centralized, urban environment. The Bauhaus Dessau chose this area when they decided to relocate from Berlin, because the leaders were convinced that Dessau had the right client base for the new modern era in the form of the enlightened functionalistic industrialist.

When, after the Second World War, Germany was divided, Dessau and its surrounding landscape came under socialist rule. A state-organized mass production of coal and minerals, as well as chemical plants and housing for the needed workers, started immediately after the socialist takeover on a much larger scale than ever before. Bitterfeld-Wolfen, located ten miles south of Dessau, became the new center, which housed the larger coal facilities and many extremely polluting chemical plants. Small rural towns were relocated

Infrastructure deflected through fields of
inhabitants' influence

into one large mass-produced housing compound of 35,000 inhabitants erected as a true machine to live in. There was no particular infrastructure, urban function, or relationship to the surrounding landscape. The machine was thought of as a storage tank for the workers employed in the coal fields and chemical industry located around the housing area. The housing of Wolfen Nord was a truly modern compound organized around the distinctly functional requirement of storing workers during the night. Few shopping amenities were added. The children were all taken care of in public daycare centers distributed within the compound. There were no other additional programs, which would support social or otherwise publicly uncontrolled gatherings, creative possibilities of appropriation, or leisure activities. Eventually the state allowed two program additions, a garage cooperative and small allotment gardens, which were heavily used by the inhabitants.

When Germany was reunited in 1990, the state-organized industries had to enter the global market. All of the existing chemical plants in the area eventually closed; all coal and mineral fields were abandoned. The Wolfen Nord housing compound went from 35,000 to 24,000 inhabitants within a few years. Whoever was able to leave left immediately. Unemployment was at fifty-five percent in 1999. Most women were out of work and the childbirth rate dropped to thirty percent. The area turned out to be one of the most problematic of the former East Germany.

Those who remained in Wolfen Nord spent most of their time in the small self-organized garage or garden compounds where alternative production slowly emerged. Numerous garden allotment organizations, where resistance to a life of uselessness was reorganized, surfaced and the garage compounds around the housing area started to support small creative activities. A culture developed of building "hotrods," making marmalade, growing flowers, and drinking excessive amounts of coffee and alcohol.

After many statistical studies and interviews, as well as surveys of the area, one particular goal emerged. Wolfen Nord needed an animation of social dynamics based on the small activities that had developed in its periphery. Structures that rearranged material, created small dynamic production units, and reacted consciously to the contemporary spatial condition, which quickly moved from the Iron Age to the Electronic Age, had to be invented. Infrastructure that made oscillating small activities more decentralized in the periphery had to be developed; small activities could be used as attractors.

This paradigm shift had very grave implications for a possible design process. Systems of distinction—such as center versus periphery, city versus landscape, architecture versus infrastructure, public versus private, author versus consumer, reality versus simulation—started to melt for us in the studio. The

The art of reusing; "hotrods" in Denmark

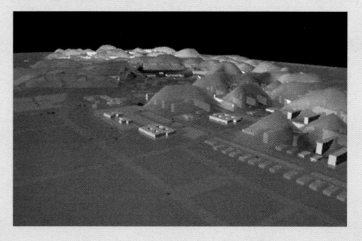

top: Activity of inhabitants at 11:00 a.m.
bottom: Activity of inhabitants at 9:00 p.m.

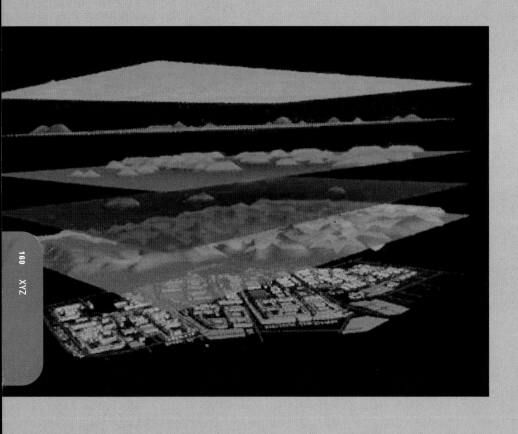

Overlapped fields of influence at different times

area we studied began to represent many realities simultaneously. The found structure had become a pulsating, permanently transforming organism that was simultaneously shrinking.

We tried to experiment with abstraction and representation by defining new or familiar ways to diagram what we saw and collected. We started to rethink the role of the diagram in a design process by reconsidering its analytical role and its role as inspiration. The diagram was first and foremost used to structure our thoughts, to abstract dynamic fields, and to translate found materials into novel combinations.

We tried to find forms of resistance and look critically upon the diagram as a tool of rhetorical backup and as a sign for things to come, as Deleuze and Guattari described it in their definition of diagrams.[4] An open network of connections and weavings needed to be established. We tried to use the collected material as a base for discursive interpretation. New data-landscapes, a kind of topology of transformative intelligence that gave us insight into multiple temporal, social, and physical dynamics, needed to be established.

4 "The diagrammatic or abstract machine does not function to represent, even something real, but rather constructs a real that is yet to come, a new type of reality. Thus when it constitutes points of creation or potentiality it does not stand outside of history but is instead always 'prior' to history." Gilles Deleuze and Félix Guattari, *A Thousand Plateaus: Capitalism and Schizophrenia*, trans. Brian Massumi (Minneapolis: University of Minnesota Press, 1987), 142.

We collected statistical material on Wolfen Nord and concentrated on particular aspects of work, consumption, social gathering, and movement. On top of the given site we modeled a mental skin that distinguished different types of action. We recorded public buildings like schools, the placement of super-markets, the density of inhabitants as density potential, movement patterns between the different centers of action, and, particularly, sites of active appropriation of pre-givens (such as gardens and garages). There we could observe leisurely appropriation of technocratic and scriptural strategies by the remainders of inhabitants, which we intended to strengthen.

The different electronic landscapes showed types of dynamic flows at the site, which we measured in connection with attractors and networkings. We made the decision that a center of action should be able to trigger dynamic movements along which basic infrastructural offerings could be placed. Our hope was to create a decentralized pattern of consumption and appropriative production along the infrastructural loops, where a network of temporary as well as long-term activities should dock.[5]

5 "In reality, a rationalized, centralized, spectacular and clamorous production is confronted by an entirely different kind of production, called consumption and characterized by its ruses, its fragmentation (the result of the circumstances), its poaching, its clandestine nature, its tireless but quiet activity, in short by its quasi-invisibility, since it shows itself not in its products

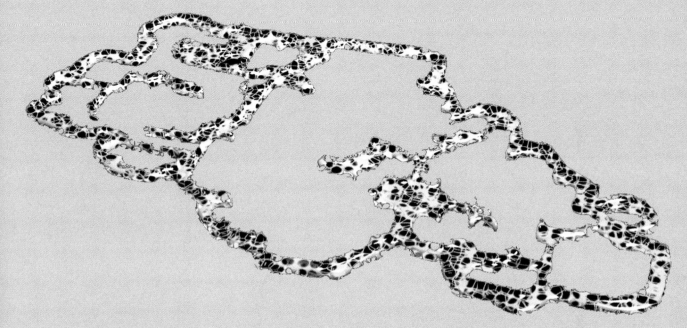

Resulting potentiality sponge

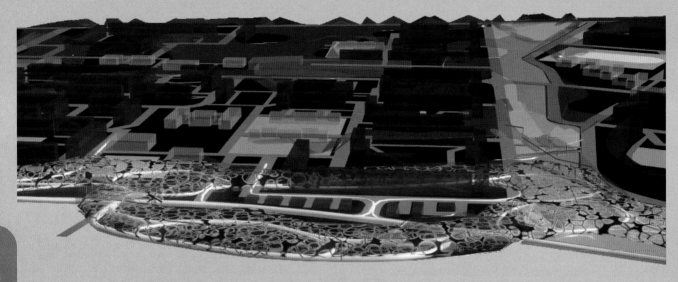

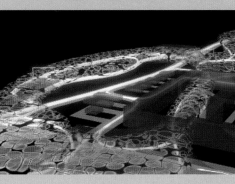

We concentrated on the existing housing and tried to add new, different structures to help reinterpret the idea of context. We created strategies to support the art of daily life with a flexible structure based on our new research on how to use interactive diagrams. We developed a structure in one fragment in order to study the infrastructural tissue more in depth. One condition that needs to be stressed here is that there should always be a clear distinction between a so-called meshwork, which operates as a dynamic three-dimensional diagram, and an intended building, which will always be normative and will move at a much slower speed.

1 PRODUCED IN 1999
Principal: Dagmar Richter
Assistants: Jonas Luther and
Michael Filser

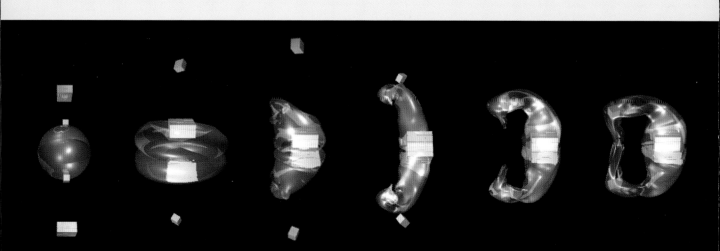

EUCLIDEAN VERSUS FLUID

During my construction of a critical and academic practice I have used open international competitions as a testing ground for my concepts and research. The following project is the result of my first invitation to enter a design competition.

The symbolism of the proposed structure is based on the idea that two distinct ordering systems and modes of thought govern the two millennia that coincide at the year 2000. We chose to represent these two systems in the cube and the fluid form.

The last one thousand years were marked by society's struggle to define the individual as a rational, singular entity. This history is dominated by the painful conflict of different ethnic groups driven by the perception of difference and a desire for separation. This struggle is at its high point. With the Second World War in living memory, genocide and ethnic cleansing remain in the news. This cultural phenomenon has been reflected in the ordering systems of artistic and architectural representation through history. Analytical drawings of Gothic cathedrals, Renaissance studies of human proportion, Le Corbusier's modular, and the proportions of film, television, and computer screens are all based on variations of the rectangle, the golden section, and the cube.[2] A cube, articulated by classical proportions, is used to represent the ordering systems and notions of beauty of the last millennium.

If any predictions would be possible for the next millennium, they would be for a new and growing interest in the concepts of meltable and fluid ordering systems.[3] Travel, immigration, and a tolerance of unfamiliar customs will increasingly make it possible for many different groups to peacefully coexist. Family units themselves have developed fluid and nomadic structures. Genetic structures are analyzed and morphed anew. Presently, it is considered possible to construct one's biography and beauty independent from family and ethnic history. Inevitably, technological and biological innovations will usher in a new age where distinctions between individual identities are less significant. Individual authorship, singular ordering systems, idealized geometrical representations, and timeless and static material conditions would all be called into question.[4] This new age is represented in the fluid sculpture of glass where two cubes float inside. The shape was produced with the help of a three-dimensional animation program where a small cube was dropped into a fluid sphere[6]

2 The relationship of the grid and straight line in opposition of the free curve and meandering line has been beautifully discussed by Catherine Ingraham: "The technical realm of architecture is, of course, mathematical and geometrical. The geometric line, in particular—that cool, rigorous line drawn on, or rather, cut into, the blankness of white paper—is the most seductive perhaps of all architectural tools. This line, which we know cannot be just a line, is iconographic in the sense that it sets in motion an entire range of practices." Catherine Ingraham, "Animals 2:

The Problem of Distinction", *Assemblage* 14 (April 1991), 26–27.
3 See Marshall Berman, *All that is Solid Melts into Air: The Experience of Modernity* (New York: Penguin, 1988).
4 "In a book, as in all things, there are lines of articulation or segmentarity, strata and territories: but also lines of flight, movements of deterritorialization and destratification. Comparative rates of flow on these lines produce phenomena of relative slowness and viscosity, or on the contrary, of acceleration and rupture." Gilles Deleuze and Félix

Guattari, *A Thousand Plateaus: Capitalism and Schizophrenia*, trans. Brian Massumi (Minneapolis: University of Minnesota Press, 1987), 3–4.

Footnote project: Ordering Systems of Los Angeles
In this project we analyzed the ordering system of Los Angeles between the flat and the hill sites. The streets and ordering systems on the flat sites were then copied and cut into the hillside in order to integrate some production units. We compared the freeway systems

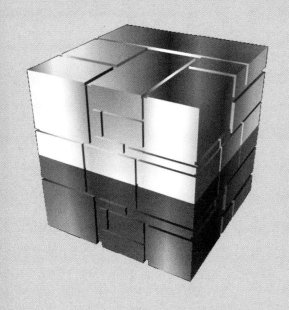

that directly reacted to the needed flow with
the hill site street system, which reacted to
the given topography. This project represents
a simple switch of the two ordering conditions.
Project Credits:
Produced in 1989
Principals: Dagmar Richer and Ulrich
Hinrichsmeyer
Assistant: Brigitte Neudahm

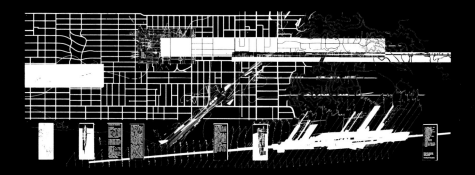

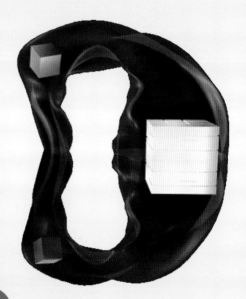

Footnote Project: Fluid Structure in the 70s
As a student of Frei Otto in 1979, I studied fluid
forms in the experiments shown here.

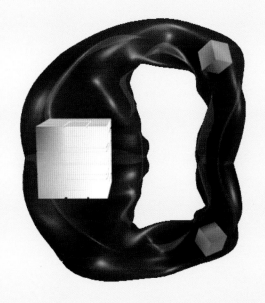

To make the capsule, classically proportioned Cupaloy metal containers would be packed side by side into one half-cube form, 3'x3'x1'. A planned visual effect would allow the physical half-cube to be mirrored and appear as a completed whole in space. Since the contents of the capsule remained undecided at the time of the competition, the variously proportioned compartments would later be coordinated to the selected objects of cultural representation. The documents and other materials would be wrapped individually in cloth before being sealed. A fluid shape of cast glass would wrap the cube almost entirely and leave only its lower face exposed. This surface would be engraved with messages relating the purpose of the object and instructions for when and how to open it. After all the boxes are in place and the air has been removed, nitrogen would be injected, and a pre-cooled metal plug in the shape of a very large screw would be threaded into place with a small amount of grease. When temperatures equalized, the entire collection of individual boxes would be tightly enclosed in a one-inch-thick metal half-cube.

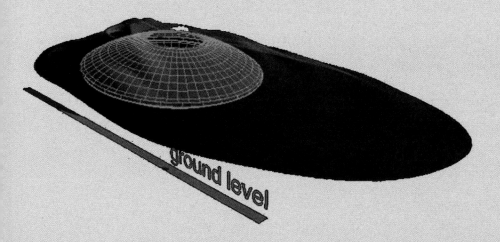

ground level

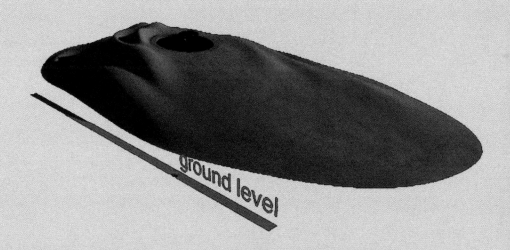

ground level

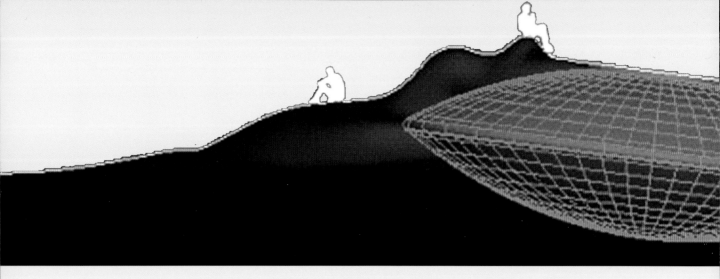

A second, smaller cube, one cubic foot in volume, would also be enclosed, floating in the glass capsule. This cube would contain a collection of as many hair samples of different New Yorkers as practical, creating a DNA Noah's Arc of the city.

The glass sculpture would be placed in an oval volume with an entirely mirrored interior surface. The resultant visual effect of double mirroring would allow a visitor peering through the top of a window at an angle of about forty-five degrees to see the glass sculpture appear three-dimensionally above the window's surface, like a hologram. The sculpture, located safely underground, would be virtually present above. It could be seen from all sides or even walked through. The window's perimeter would be engraved with the date of 1 January 2000, as well as all of the corresponding dates of non-Christian calendars.

We chose a grassy area in Central Park near the rock formations at Cleopatra's Needle as the capsule's site. The proposed surrounding landscape consists of sculptural, soft shapes covered with mossy vegetation and used for sunbathing, picnicking, and contemplation. Its contours would provide several possible viewing elevations. The needle, itself several thousand years old, would cast a shadow on the capsule's window on New Years Day.

Cleopatra's Needle

We planned two varieties of time capsules. We regard the one in Central Park, we regard as the original. Located in a prominent public space, it commemorates the event of the year 2000, it is a reminder of time, and it is a small peace memorial. This original is not necessary, however, for the practical storage of the information. The contents are largely symbolic, the intent being to place the capsule within the collective conscience of the contemporary culture.

A fixed number of copies of the capsule would be simultaneously manufactured in miniature form. These would be identical to the original, but at one-twelfth its scale. They would contain the same shaped glass sculpture, which would enclose a small cube of a 3x1.5'' cavity and a very small second cube for hair samples. The contents of the original would be reproduced in the copies on HD-Rosetta disks, smaller than 2.5 inches in diameter. These copies would then be distributed among institutions such as the Museum of Natural History, the *New York Times* offices, the Museum of Modern Art, and the United Nations, among others. These miniature capsules would be used in public displays to produce a visual effect similar to the original. Private individuals would also be allowed to purchase copies and add hair samples of their family into the second cube. Owners would receive an optical microscope, instructions, and a list of contents. Each would bear the responsibility of passing the

capsule on to the next generation until the scheduled opening in the year 3000. Based on the sale of these multiples, the *New York Times* will be able to finance the entire endeavor.

Beyond the construction of the large public memorial in Central Park, we suggested two additional burial sites for the smaller version of the container. One possible site was located at Battery Park, where numerous smaller war memorials are located between the Museum of Jewish Heritage and the Castle Clinton National Monument, with a good view of the Statue of Liberty. The smaller version of the capsule would have an eight-inch diameter window and roughly the same scale as the surrounding memorials. Placed here, it would critically remind us of the troubles of a one-thousand-year frame of reference; the One-Thousand-Year Reich is an example from history. A second possible site lay among the small traffic islands at Times Square. Since the capsule's window is planned to be flush with the ground and rather small, there would be little disruption of foot traffic. Here the reference would be commercial and colorful, the capsule functioning as an event associated with New Year's festivities.

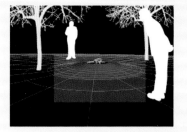

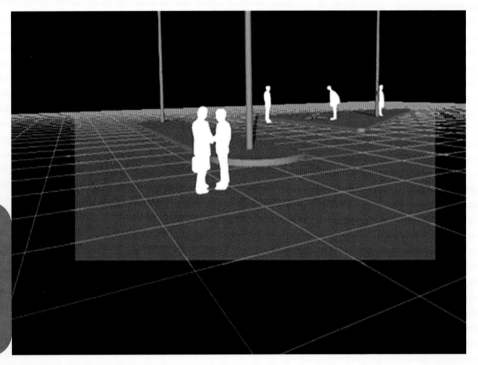

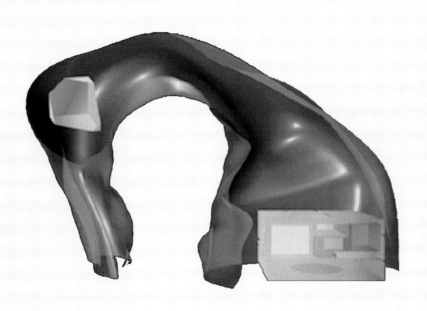

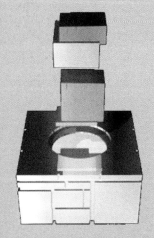

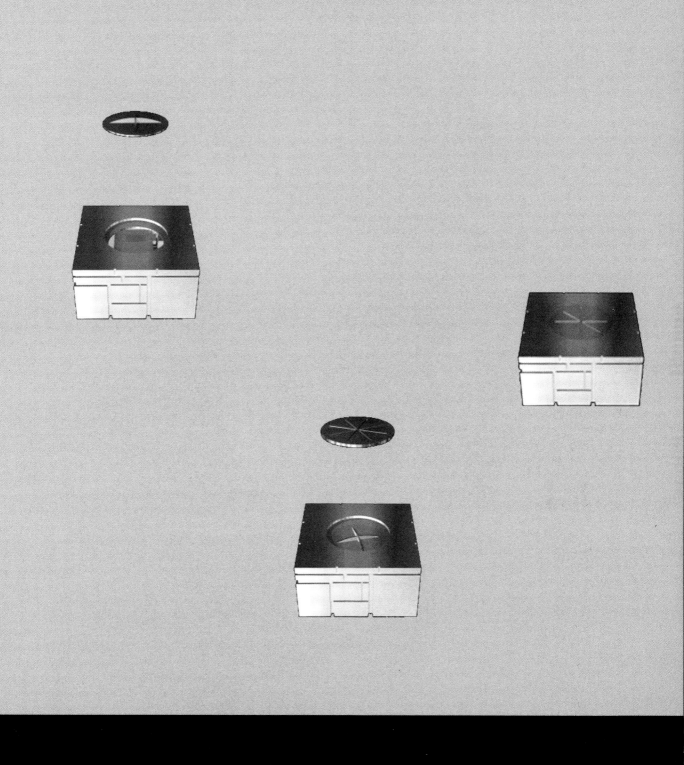

DAGMAR RICHTER

CHRONOLOGY

1984 Invited Housing for Regensburg Competition
With: Liza Hansen for Gehrdt Bornebusch, Copenhagen

PRIZE: First

EXHIBITED: Royal Art Academy, Copenhagen, 1985

PUBLISHED: *Arkitekten* 12, 1984
                Baumeister 1, 1985
                Arkitekten DK 21/22, 1986

1984 International UNESCO Competition:
City of the Future
With: Peter Lunding

PRIZE: First Denmark

EXHIBITED: UIFA and IBA, Berlin, 1984

PUBLISHED: *Arkitekten*, June 1984 Pedersen Jakob, ed.
                Ung Arkitektur, Copenhagen 1986

1985 International Copenhagen Harbor Competition

PRIZE: Mention

EXHIBITED: Galerie Wolf-Raeune, Düsseldorf, 1985

PUBLISHED: *Arkitekten* 15, 1985 Pedersen Jakob, ed.
                Ung Arkitektur. Copenhagen, 1986
                A+U 233, February 1990

1985 Gate for Paestum Project

EXHIBITED: Galerie Wolf-Raeune, Düsseldorf, 1985
Projects by Selected Postgraduate Students of the
Städel Schule, a traveling exhibition of outstanding
work from the Städel School, 1987–88: Museum for
Modern Art, Kassel; Cooper Union, New York; Skala
Galleri, Copenhagen; Deutsches Architektur Museum,
Frankfurt/Main; AEDES Gallerie, Berlin

PUBLISHED: *AD: Architectural Design,* May 1985
Scala 3, May 1986
Arkitekten 6, March 1988
A+U 233, February 1990

1985 Wall of Kassel Project

EXHIBITED: Galerie Wolf-Raeune, Düsseldorf, 1985
Projects by Selected Postgraduate Students of the
Städel Schule, a traveling exhibition of outstanding
work from the Städel School, 1987–88: Museum for
Modern Art, Kassel; Cooper Union, New York; Skala
Galleri, Copenhagen; Deutsches Architektur Museum,
Frankfurt/Main; AEDES Gallerie, Berlin

PUBLISHED: *Arkitekten* 8, 1987
Arkitekten 6, 1988
A+U 233, February 1990

1986 Berlin 3 Project
With: Ulrich Hinrichsmeyer

EXHIBITED: "Berlin: Denkmal oder Denkmodell?,"
Kunsthalle Berlin, 1988
Gallery ROM, Oslo, Norway, 1988
"Ulrich Hinrichsmeyer and Dagmar Richter," Gallerie
Fenster, Frankfurt, 1990
StoreFront for Art and Architecture, New York, 1992
"The Art of Copy," GSAUP Gallery at UCLA,
Los Angeles, 1993

PUBLISHED: Kristin Feireiss, *Berlin: Denkmal oder Denkmodell?,*
Berlin, 1988
A+U 233, February 1990
Aaron Betsky. *Violated Perfection.*
New York: Rizzoli, 1990

1987 Shinkenshiku, Central Glass
International Competition
With: Ulrich Hinrichsmeyer

PRIZE: Second

EXHIBITED: Gallery ROM, Oslo, 1988
Gallery Skala, Copenhagen, 1988
Gallerie Fenster, Frankfurt am Main, 1990

PUBLISHED: *JA,* January 1988
A+U 233, February 1990

1987 Women's Rights National Historic Park Competition
EXHIBITED: Gallery Skala, Copenhagen, 1988

PUBLISHED: *Arkitekt Nytt,* April 1988
A+U 233, February 1990

1987 Boston National Artist's Housing Competition

    EXHIBITED: Gallery ROM, Oslo, 1988
                  Gallery Skala, Copenhagen, 1988

    PUBLISHED: *Arkitekten* 6 March 1988
                  Arkitekt Nytt, April 1988
                  A+U 233, February 1990

1988 West Coast Gateway Competition
With: Shayne O'Neil

    ASSISTANTS: *FIRST PHASE:* Thomas Robertson;
                  SECOND PHASE: David Adler, Roger Fairey, Eric Lum,
                  Anthony Poon, Thomas Robertson

    PRIZE: *FIRST PHASE:* finalist; *SECOND PHASE:* third prize

    EXHIBITED: Gallery ROM, Oslo, 1988
                  Gallery Skala, Copenhagen, 1988
                  "Current Exhibition," Harvard University GSD, 1989

    PUBLISHED: *Werk Bauen Wohnen*, 8 July 1990
                  A+U 233, February 1990
                  Assemblage 14, 1991
                  Journal of Philosophy and the Visual Arts,
                  London, 2, 1992
                  Maggie Toy, ed. *World Cities: Los Angeles.* London:
                  Academy Editions, 1994
                  Francesca Hughes, ed. *The Architect: Reconstructing*
                  Her Practice. Cambridge. MA: MIT Press,1996

1989 Shinkenshiku International Housing Competition
With: Ulrich Hinrichsmeyer
Assistant: Brigitte Neudahm

    EXHIBITED: Gallery Skala, Copenhagen, 1988

    PUBLISHED: *Assemblage* 14, 1991

1989 International Competition for
The German Broadcasting Museum
Assistants: Liza Hansen, Petra Larsen, Tom Robertson

    EXHIBITED: GSAUP Gallery, UCLA, 1989

1989–90 Child's Guesthouse
Assistants: Claudia Lueling and Joshua Levine
Engineer: Mike Ischler

    EXHIBITED: StoreFront for Art and Architecture, New York, 1992
                  National AIA Convention, Los Angeles, 1994
                  Contemporary Architect Exhibition, Nara, Japan, 1995
                  Staedtebau Anderswo: TU, Berlin, 1995

    PUBLISHED: *Offramp* 1:4, 1991
                  Journal of Philosophy and the Visual Arts 2, 1992
                  L'Architecture d'Aujourd'Hui 290, December 1993

1990 Rebuilding Beirut: Wrapping up a War
Assistants: Anne Bolneset, Joshua Levine, Robert Thibodeau,
Theodore Zoumboulakis

    EXHIBITED: Bryce Bannantyne Gallery, Santa Monica, 1991
                  "Demarcating Lines," Urban Projects for Beirut,
                  MIT Museum, Boston, 1991
                  StoreFront for Art and Architecture, New York, 1992
                  Contemporary Architect Exhibition, Nara, Japan, 1995
                  Staedtebau Anderswo: TU, Berlin, 1995

    PUBLISHED: *Assemblage* 14, 1991
                  Journal of Philosophy and the Visual Arts 2, 1992
                  Francesca Hughes, ed. *The Architect: Reconstructing*
                  Her Practice. Cambridge, MA: MIT Press, 1996

1990 Re-Reading the City:

An Earthscratcher for Century City

Assistants: Anne Bolneset, Joshua Levine, Cordell Steinmetz,
Robert Thibodeau, Theodore Zoumboulakis

EXHIBITED: Bryce Bannantyne Gallery, Santa Monica, 1991
"New World Images," Louisiana Museum,
Denmark, 1992
StoreFront for Art and Architecture, New York, 1992
"Theory and Experimentation,"
Royal Institute of British Architects, London, 1992
Contemporary Architect Exhibition, Nara, Japan, 1995
Staedtebau Anderswo: TU, Berlin, 1995
Sixth Viennese Architectural Seminar, Vienna, 1995–96
Henry Urbach Gallery, New York, 1997
"Archilab," Orleans, April 1999

PUBLISHED: *Assemblage* 14, 1991
Journal of Philosophy and the Visual Arts, London, 2,
1992
Maggie Toy, ed. *World Cities: Los Angeles.* London:
Academy Editions, 1994
Francesca Hughes, ed. *The Architect: Reconstructing*
Her Practice. Cambridge, MA: MIT Press, 1996
Frederic Migayrou and Marie-Ange Brayer, ed.
Archilab. Orleans, 1999

1991 Murphy Table Prototype

Assistant: Joshua Levine

EXHIBITED: Gallery of Functional Arts, Santa Monica, 1991
StoreFront for Art and Architecture, New York, 1992

1991 Curtain and Wall House

Assistants: Hagy Belzberg, Eileen Yankowsky, Theodore Zoumboulakis
Engineer: Mike Ischler

EXHIBITED: StoreFront for Art and Architecture, New York, 1992
National AIA Convention, Los Angeles, 1994
Contemporary Architect Exhibition, Nara, Japan, 1995
Staedtebau Anderswo: TU, Berlin, 1995
Sixth Viennese Architectural Seminar, Vienna, 1995–96

PUBLISHED: *Journal of Philosophy and the Visual Arts*, 2, 1992
Maggie Toy, ed. *World Cities: Los Angeles.* London:
Academy Editions, 1994

1991–93 Devine Residence

Assistants: Eileen Yankowski and Theodore Zoumboulakis

EXHIBITED: StoreFront for Art and Architecture, New York, 1992
GSAUP Gallery at UCLA, Los Angeles, 1993
National AIA Convention, Los Angeles, 1994

PUBLISHED: *Reports* 1. New York: StoreFront for Art and
Architecture, 1991
Maggie Toy, ed. *World Cities: Los Angeles.* London:
Academy Editions, 1994

1992 International Urban Design Competition for Tbilisi

With: Ulrich Hinrichsmeyer

PRIZE: Invitation to second phase

1992 International Competition for the Extension
for the Museum of Fine Arts, Copenhagen

With: Liza Hansen

EXHIBITED: Museum of Modern Art, Copenhagen, 1992

1992 Proposal for a New Government Center in Berlin
Assistants: Joe Day, Nina Lesser, Jonathan Massey, Carola Sapper, Patrick Tighe

EXHIBITED: Columbia University, New York, 1992
              SCI-Arc , Los Angeles, 1992
              StoreFront for Art and Architecture, New York, 1992
              GSAUP Gallery at UCLA, Los Angeles, 1993
              Contemporary Architect Exhibition, Nara, Japan, 1995
              Staedtebau Anderswo: TU, Berlin, 1995
              Sixth Viennese Architectural Seminar, 1995–96

PUBLISHED: Andreas Müller and Ria Stein, ed. *Hauptstadt Berlin-Parlamentsviertel im Spreebogen: International Competition for Urban Ideas 1993.* Berlin: Birkhäuser Verlag, 1993
              Assemblage 29, 1996

1993 New Royal Library, Copenhagen, Denmark
Assistants: Nick Capelli, Mercedes De La Garza, Liza Hansen, Carl Hampson, Marc Kim, Scott Oliver, Keith Sidley

PRIZE: Second

EXHIBITED: Bella Center, Copenhagen, Denmark, 1993
              GSAUP Gallery at UCLA, Los Angeles, 1993
              Staedtebau Anderswo: TU, Berlin, 1995

PUBLISHED: *Arkitekten* 16, 1993
              Zodiac 11, March–August 1994
              OZ 16, 1994
              Francesca Hughes, ed. *The Architect: Reconstructing Her Practice.* Cambridge, MA: MIT Press, 1996

1993 Shinkenshiku Membrane Competition
Assistants: Michael Brem, Sam Sheppert, and Gudrun Wiedemer

PRIZE: First

EXHIBITED: Staedtebau Anderswo: TU, Berlin, 1995

PUBLISHED: *Shinkenchiku* 11, 1994
              Angelika Schnell, Young German Architects. Basel: Birkhäuser Verlag, 2000.

1996 Shanghai Residential Design 2000 Competition
Assistants: Justin DeWitt, Behnam Samareh, and Denise Zacky

EXHIBITED: "Collaborations," Hollyhock Gallery, Los Angeles, 1997
              Archilab, Orleans, April 1999

PUBLISHED: *Newsline*, Columbia University, New York, spring 1997
              Frederic Migayrou and Marie-Ange Brayer, ed. *Archilab.* Orleans, 1999

1997 Fine Arts Seismic Facility at UC Riverside
(Design Consultant)
With: Israel Callas Shortridge (Design Architects) and Annie Chu (Project Designer)

PRIZE: "AIA Next LA," 1997

EXHIBITED: "Collaborations," Hollyhock Gallery, Los Angeles, 1997

1997–98 A House on Top of a House
Assistant: Gudrun Wiedemer
EXHIBITED: National AIA Convention, Los Angeles, 1998

1997–98 Planning Model for Manhattan

Assistants: Amber Evans, Maria-Jose Riera, Justin Rumpeles, Behnam Samareh, and Curtis Simmons

EXHIBITED: Archilab, April 1999

PUBLISHED: Frederic Migayrou and Marie-Ange Brayer, ed. *Archilab*. Orleans, 1999

1999 New York Time's Millennium Capsule Competition

Assistants: Jonas Luther and Michael Filser

PRIZE: Finalist

EXHIBITED: "Winners of the The New York Times Millennium Competition," Museum of Natural History, New York, 1999–2000
"New York Times Millennium Competition," Architecture Gallery of UCLA, Los Angeles, 2000

PUBLISHED: *New York Times Magazine*, 5 December 1999
Angelika Schnell, *Young German Architects*. Basel: Birkhäuser Verlag, 2000.

1998–99 Wolfen Nord: A Model for a New Planning Case Study

Assistant: Jonas Luther

EXHIBITED: Internationales Forum, Ulm, 1999

PUBLISHED: *Strategic Space: Urbanity in the Twenty-first Century.* Ulm: Anabas Verlag, 2000
Angelika Schnell, *Young German Architects*. Basel: Birkhäuser Verlag, 2000.

2000 Research Project for a Dwelling

EXHIBITED: "Live Dangerously," Armand Hammer Museum, Los Angeles, 2000

Writings by Dagmar Richter

"Haus Schnabel, Los Angeles 1988." *Werk Bauen Wohnen,* Zurich. 8 July 1990: 34–58.

"Architectural Design Theory, Education and Practice." *Square*, San Francisco (May–June 1992): 7.

"The Art of Copy: Experiments for Adequate Space Creation in the Public Space." *The Empty Space, The Public Space.* Vienna: Springer Wien, 1995–96, 130–141.

"Spazieren in Berlin." *Assemblage* 29. Cambridge, MA: MIT Press, 1996, 72–85.

"Ueber den Ort, den Autor und den Ethos der Reinlichkeit." Trans. Benedikt Kraft. DBZ 8 (1996): 87–89.

"Flow Versus Boundary: Andrew Zago." *DAIDALOS* 71: 86–91.

"The Glass Ceiling." *MA MA* 26 (2000): 48–49.

Major Publications on Dagmar Richter

"Reading Los Angeles: A Primitive Rebel's Account." *Assemblage* 14 (1991): 66–81.

"The Art of Copy," *Journal of Philosophy and the Visual Arts* 2 (1992): 45–53.

Andreas Papadakis, ed. *Theory and Experimentation.* London: Academy Editions, 1993, 1, 49, 50, 64, 342–355.

Contemporary Architect Exhibition II. Nara, Japan, 1995.

Francesca Hughes, ed. "A Practice of One's Own." *The Architect: Reconstructing Her Practice.* Cambridge, MA: MIT Press, 1996, 96–126.

Angelika Schnell, *Young German Architects.* Basel: Birkhäuser Verlag, 2000, 78–87.

Joerg Kirchbaum and Anna Meseure, ed. *International Forum Prague: Architecture and Responsibility.* Vienna: Arcum Verlag, 1997, 185–201.